TASTY
TONY SINGH

FOOD THAT GIVES YOU
A HUG AND
MAKES YOU SMILE

headline

First published in 2014
by HEADLINE PUBLISHING GROUP

1

Cataloguing in Publication Data is available from the British Library

Hardback ISBN 9781472219084

Project editor: Imogen Fortes
Design: Pene Parker
Photography and prop styling: Haarala Hamilton
Illustrations: Grace Helmer
Food styling: Kat Mead and Nicole Herft

Printed and bound in Italy by Rotolito Lombarda SpA.

HEADLINE PUBLISHING GROUP
An Hachette UK Company
338 Euston Road
London NW1 3BH

www.headline.co.uk
www.hachette.co.uk

CONTENTS

Tasty
adjective

1. (Of food) having a pleasant, distinct flavour:

'*a tasty snack*'

Synonyms

Delicious, palatable, luscious, mouth-watering, delectable, toothsome, succulent, juicy.

www.oxforddictionaries.com

Chaat

A Punjabi/Hindi word meaning 'tasting', 'a delicacy', 'to lick', 'to devour with relish', 'to eat noisily'. (This is my understanding of the word but it's different in some dialects throughout India.)

These are the two words that sum up my attitude to food. They mean more to me than what is hot in the ever-changing, fast-paced world of today's restaurant scene; what is being tweeted or blogged about; or adhering to any particular style of cooking. Food is about taste. It's about flavour, it's about that bit of TLC you put into the dishes you are making for someone or even that TLC you show yourself by knocking something together instead of picking up a microwave meal or calling for a takeaway (not that I don't do that once in a while too).

The point I'm making is that tasty cooking, tasty food doesn't have to mean spending hours slaving over a stove. It can be had from opening a tin of beans, cooking them with a simple Holy Trinity of garlic, chilli and ginger, then serving them with some toast. No, that's not gourmet, it's not grand, but you have a very quick supper, one that you have cooked yourself, and most importantly, it's tasty (trust me – it's so good, I've even included the recipe, on page 26).

I repeat: you will have cooked. Detractors will be saying that this is not cooking, that jazzed-up beans is too easy, that cooking should be hard; it should require effort and anxiety, time and precision. Well, I say what a load of mince – and not the tasty type. Tasty food is not, and should not, be scary or hard. Any good ingredients, whether fresh or processed, combined with care and thought will result in a tasty dish. Of course you can cook complex recipes and try different techniques; there's no doubt this has amazing results, but cooking and eating are above all about fun.

Tasty is a book for cooks and for anybody wanting to have a go at cooking. It is not a book with complicated techniques, nor is it fashion-led. It's taste-led. It's the food I cook for my friends, family and guests.

You may be surprised to see some convenience foods in the book – from Swiss rolls and gingerbread to shop-bought mayonnaise and custard. If you want to make these ingredients, that's wonderful – and in some cases, I've given you the recipes so that you can do so – but if you're strapped for time, there is nothing wrong with using the best ready-prepared ingredients you can find. After all, what we want at the end of our efforts is a tasty dish and happy tums; how you get there just isn't as important.
We can all use words and fancy ingredients to our heart's content, but there's nothing more rewarding and powerful at mealtimes than displays of the truly international language in food: an appreciative tummy pat, the 'mmmms' and 'ahhhs', the smiles on people's lips and their clean plates speak so much louder than words, and for me that's what it's all about; that's why I cook.

So, dive in: learn from your mistakes, celebrate your triumphs and enjoy every last lip-smacking mouthful.

Tony Singh

> *'The only real stumbling block is fear of failure.*
> *In cooking you've got to have a what-the-hell attitude.'*
>
> Julia Child

01 MUNCHIES

When hunger strikes, you become ravenous and you need to scratch that itch, it's to this chapter you need to turn.

I have put together a few of my favourite itch-scratchers, all of them easy to prepare, that will satisfy different snack desires — sweet, salty and spicy — and accompany a cold beer or a mid-afternoon cup of tea.

Most are light and aimed at filling a small hole so they shouldn't spoil your appetite later. Some, however, are really rib-sticking: my God's own bacon roll, Desperate Dan beans and the American dream pancakes aren't going to leave much room for anything else, but they're all lifesavers when an attack of the munchies strikes.

Lime almonds

You can use any kind of nut in this recipe – cashews, hazelnuts or walnuts would be just as good, but peel them if you can as the skins can sometimes have a bitterness. Lime – or lemon juice if you prefer – is a great partner for nuts: the sharpness of the citrus contrasts with the richness of the nut. It might sound strange to soak the nuts for so long, but the longer you leave them the more flavour they take on.

Serves 4–6 as a nibble with drinks

200g whole almonds, peeled if possible
150ml lime juice
3 tbsp olive oil
1 tsp mango powder (amchoor)
1½ tsp sea salt (optional)

1 Spread the almonds out in a shallow dish, pour in the lime juice and mix well so the nuts are well coated. Leave for 8 hours, turning them every time you remember.

2 Preheat the oven to 180°C/gas 4.

3 Drain the almonds, then spread them out on a baking tray and bake for around 10 minutes, turning them every 2 minutes.

4 In a bowl mix the oil and mango powder then tip in the hot almonds. Mix well then place the nuts back on the baking tray and return to the oven for a further 10 minutes, or until golden brown. Stir though the salt, if using, leave to cool and then munch. The almonds will keep for a week in an airtight tub. If they feel like they are going soft, a quick flash in a hot oven will sort them out.

Caramel spiced nuts

These caramelised spiced nuts are sweet, salty, savoury and spicy
– all the things you want in a nibble… and they help the beer go down!

Serves 8–10 as a nibble with drinks

75g dark or light muscovado sugar
1 tsp ground cinnamon
1 tsp five-spice powder
½ tsp chilli powder
1 egg white
200g almonds
200g cashews

1. Preheat oven to 150°C/gas 2. Line a baking tray with greaseproof paper or a silicone mat.

2. In a medium bowl, combine the sugar and spices.

3. In a large bowl, whisk together the egg white and 1 tablespoon of water until frothy and fairly stiff. Add the nuts then stir in the sugar mixture until the nuts are evenly coated. Spread the nuts out on the prepared tray in a single layer. Bake for 15 minutes.

4. Give the nuts a good stir then bake for a further 15 minutes. They should be golden brown and smell divine – if they are still a bit light, pop them back in the oven. Leave to cool completely.

Muttia

These crispy little bread fritters that are served all over India are such a moreish nibble. They are great dipped in sweet milky tea – munch on them as they go soggy – or just try them straight up. The ajwain seeds give them a wee kick.

Serves 6–8 as a snack with drinks

250g plain flour
1 tsp fine table salt
1 tsp ajwain seeds
2 tbsp rapeseed oil
about 100ml warm water
vegetable oil, for deep-frying

1 Mix the flour, salt and ajwain seeds in a large bowl. Add the rapeseed oil and rub it in to make breadcrumbs. Make a well in the middle of the mix and pour in 100ml of warm water. Bring it to a dough and knead till smooth and elastic (if you need to add more water, add just a wee bit at a time), then divide the dough into four.

2 Very lightly flour a work surface then roll out one piece of dough to about 2mm thick; don't use too much flour. Traditionally, the dough is cut into diamonds but you can just cut it into 5 x 7cm strips if you prefer.

3 Put a deep-fat fryer on to 165°C or fill a deep pan a quarter full with oil and heat. To check it's ready, toss in a piece of dough. If it starts fizzing, the oil is hot enough.

4 Once the oil is hot, deep-fry the strips in small batches till golden brown. Lift out with a slotted spoon and drain on kitchen paper. Now roll out the remaining pieces of dough and fry the remaining batches. Serve once they have cooled down. Store in an airtight container for up to a week.

Popcorn

Show me someone who doesn't like popcorn and I'll convert them. Popcorn is a great vehicle for loads of flavours, and once you know how to make it (this recipe is so easy), the sky's the limit – sweet, savoury, savoury and sweet mixed together, spicy... What about some buttered caramel poured over it? Or truffle oil and Parmesan? Or some chilli and a bit of lime on top? Go crazy!

Serves 4

2 tbsp oil (you need to use an oil with a high smoking point, like rapeseed or peanut oil)
100g popping corn
seasoning of your choice, such as salt, sugar, Ras El Hanout (see page 245), grated Parmesan and truffle oil or the spice mix below

Popcorn spice mix

2 tbsp coriander seeds
2 tbsp cumin seeds
1 tbsp caraway seeds
1 tbsp chilli flakes
1 tbsp pomegranate powder or ½ tbsp mango powder (amchoor); both are available at Asian food shops but if you can't get either toss through the juice from 1 lime just before you add the rest of the spice mix

1. If you're preparing the popcorn spice mix, start with that. Toast the seeds and chilli flakes in a dry frying pan over a low–medium heat, stirring constantly, until they give off a fragrant aroma. Remove from the pan and set aside to cool.

2. Mix in the pomegranate powder or mango powder. Whizz the mixture briefly in a grinder or pound in a mortar and pestle.

3. For the popcorn, heat the oil in a very large pan over a medium–high heat. Put three or four corn kernels into the oil and cover the pan with a lid. When the kernels pop, add the rest of the popcorn in an even layer, cover with a lid, then take off the heat and count 30 seconds.

4. Return the pan to the heat and the popcorn will begin popping. Gently shake the pan by moving it back and forth over the heat. Once the popping slows to several seconds between pops, remove the pan from the heat, remove the lid, and transfer the popcorn immediately to a wide bowl. Season with your choice of seasoning and serve.

Duck wontons

These are great as a nibble, a canapé or if you poach them in a broth, a super base for a hearty noodle broth.

Makes 20 wontons

2 duck legs, meat taken off the bone
   and minced or roughly blitzed
   in a food processor
4 rashers of unsmoked streaky bacon,
   roughly blitzed in a food processor
4 shallots, thinly sliced
1 tbsp hoisin sauce
1 tsp finely grated fresh ginger
1 garlic clove, crushed
½ hot green chilli, finely chopped
1 tbsp chopped coriander
about 20 wonton wrappers
1 egg, beaten
vegetable oil, for deep-frying
Thai Dipping Sauce (see page 118),
   to serve

1 Put the duck meat, bacon, shallots, hoisin sauce, ginger, garlic, chilli and coriander into a medium bowl and mix well.

2 Place 2 teaspoons of the duck mixture on a corner of a wonton wrapper. Brush the edges lightly with beaten egg. Fold the corner and sides over the filling, then press the edges firmly together to seal. Repeat with the remaining mixture and wrappers.

3 Put a deep-fat fryer on to 165°C or fill a deep pan a quarter full with oil and heat. Test it's hot enough by tossing in a cube of bread – it should sizzle immediately. Deep-fry the wontons, in batches of four, for 2–3 minutes, until golden and cooked through. Remove from the oil with a slotted spoon and drain on kitchen paper. Serve the wontons immediately with the dipping sauce.

American dream pancakes

When I am in America I love a big helping of buttermilk pancakes with bacon and maple syrup, but it's a bit of a faff to make them yourself at home as you need two or three pans on the go. So here's a wee all-in-one number that's simple yet tasty.

Serves 4

125g plain flour
1 tsp salt
1 tsp bicarbonate of soda
1 egg
250ml buttermilk
100g butter, melted, plus extra to serve
   (optional)
12 rashers of smoked streaky bacon
150ml maple syrup

1   Put a large non-stick frying pan over a medium heat so that it's nice and hot when you're ready to start cooking.

2   Mix the flour, salt and bicarbonate of soda together in a bowl, then add the egg, buttermilk and butter and mix well to combine. The batter should look thick and lush.

3   Cook the bacon in four batches – three rashers at a time – until crispy on both sides. This will leave a nice amount of tasty bacon fat in the pan. As each batch of bacon is ready, spoon a quarter of the batter into the pan, spreading it out lightly with the back of the spoon. Cook the first side till you get bubbles or holes appearing on top of the batter then flip the pancake over and cook till golden brown. Keep warm in a low oven while you cook the remaining bacon and batter.

4   When ready to serve, gently heat the maple syrup in a pan. Put the pancakes on serving plates, pour over some hot maple syrup, and add a bit of butter if you like – what the hell, in for a penny, in for a pound.

God's own bacon roll

One of my all-time favourite munches is a wee nibble the boys called 'God's own bacon roll': smoked bacon in a soft morning roll, slices of butter, a home-made tattie scone, a fried hen's egg and brown sauce! And to wash this ambrosia down, not nectar but the drink that's even better: a mug of sweet builders' tea! This is not a hard recipe; it can even just be thought of as an assembly job. The ingredients should be of the best quality you can afford, but there is nothing other-worldly about them (apart from the tattie scone, if you live down south – hence the recipe I have included).

Serves 4

8 rashers of dry-cured smoked back bacon (if you are using a more mainstream bacon that has a bit of water pumped into it, go for 3 rashers per person)
4 Scottish morning rolls (soft, round rolls)
unsalted Scottish butter, chilled
oil, for frying the eggs (I go for a neutral veg or groudnut oil)
1 Tattie scone (see page 231), cut into quarters
4 large eggs
brown sauce (I use the classic HP sauce)
salt and pepper

1 Preheat the grill to high.

2 Place the bacon on a tray and pop under the grill to cook. I like it a bit crispy on the fat but cook it as you like it – just not super crispy as you need the meat to yield to the bite.

3 Cut the rolls in half and butter the top and bottom with the cold butter. How can this be done, you say? Well, when I say butter I really mean slice the butter as thinly as possible and cover the bottom and top of the roll, then set the rolls to one side.

4 Switch the oven on low – 100°C/gas ¼. Splash a bit of oil into a heavy-based pan then add a good knob of butter and place over a medium heat. Swish the butter around the pan so it does not burn. When the butter is foaming add your quarters of tattie scone and gently cook till golden brown on one side, then flip over and do the same again (add a wee bit of butter if it is all soaked up by frying the first side). Take out and place on kitchen paper, pat off the excess fat and keep warm in the low oven.

5 Pour more oil into the pan so that it is about 1cm deep. Get it nice and hot and fry your eggs. I know everybody has their eggs their own way but trust me on this one: you want the yolk soft and runny.

6 To assemble, put a tattie scone quarter on the bottom of the roll, top with two rashers of bacon, a fried egg and a good zig-zag of brown sauce, then cover with the top of the roll and enjoy!

Desperate Dan beans

This is one for when you've really got the munchies. Nine times out of ten you've got a tin of baked beans in the house and in my house there is always going to be some garam masala and some chillies; I'd advise you to ensure the same. Just those three wonders, mixed together and fried, is fantastic, but add a wee bit of onion and some garlic and these beans become really special. Put a fried egg on top and you've got a breakfast of champions. Desperate Dan beans are also great with sausages rolls, pies or anything you want.

Serves 2

2 tbsp vegetable oil
2 small red onions, finely chopped
4 garlic cloves, finely chopped
2.5cm piece of ginger, finely chopped
1 tsp finely chopped green bird's eye
  chilli
1 tsp garam masala
150ml water
1 x 400g tin baked beans
1 tbsp chopped flat-leaf parsley
salt, to taste

1 Place the oil in a heavy-bottomed pan, fry the onions till they start to brown, then add the garlic and ginger and fry till the garlic colours. Add the chilli, garam masala and water and cook till nearly all the water has evaporated.

2 Add the beans and bring to a slow simmer. Cook for 5 minutes, then stir in the parsley and check the seasoning - you may need to add some salt. Serve immediately.

Quails' eggs

One of my friends came back from Vietnam talking about how they serve their eggs – quail, hen and duck eggs – there, and I loved the idea. Boil the eggs then dip them in a mixture of lime, chilli, coriander and salt . It's so easy and if you go for the quails' eggs they make a fabulous, sophisticated-looking wee nibble.

Serves 4

24 quails' eggs
2 serrano chillies, deseeded and finely
   chopped
juice of 4 limes
½ tbsp chopped coriander
salt

1 Bring a large pan of water to the boil then cook the eggs in two batches. Drop them into the boiling water for 2½ minutes exactly then scoop out and plunge into ice-cold water. Leave till cold. Drain the eggs and pat dry, then pop into a serving bowl.

2 Mix the chilli, lime juice, coriander and some salt together, then divide between four small bowls. Let your guests peel their own eggs, then dip and eat to their heart's content.

Or swap in ...
You can do this with small hens' eggs, just boil them for 7 minutes.

Cauliflower and ginger pakoras with sweet red pepper and coconut chutney

This is a great way to use up leftover cauliflower or in fact any veg; it works well with broccoli or asparagus. The chutney can be kept in the fridge for three or four days and used as a dip for the Muttia (see page 16), Duck Wontons (see page 22) or a lovely piece of grilled fish.

Makes 24 (to serve about 12)

½ small cauliflower, broken into small
   florets
1 large red onion, peeled and sliced
1 carrot, peeled and cut into 5cm
   matchsticks
½ red pepper, sliced into 5cm
   matchsticks
1 tbsp chopped coriander
1½ tsp garam masala
¼ tsp chilli powder
1 tsp salt
200g gram flour
vegetable oil, for frying
Sweet Red Pepper and
   Coconut Chutney (see page 238),
   to serve

1 Place all the prepared vegetables in a large bowl. Add the chopped coriander, spices and salt and mix well. Leave for 5 minutes.

2 Add the gram flour to the bowl and mix well, then add 3 or 4 teaspoons of water and mix it well. You are aiming for a batter that holds the veg together. The veg should still be visible and the batter shouldn't be too wet otherwise the pakoras will not be crispy when cooked.

3 Heat 5cm of vegetable oil in a shallow pan. Test it is hot enough by throwing in a cube of bread – it should brown in about 1 minute.

4 When the oil is hot, spoon in tablespoons of the mixture until you have about five in the pan. Press down a little with the back of a spoon to flatten them slightly (they should be roughly 4cm wide) and cook on each side till golden and crispy.

5 Remove from the pan with a slotted spoon, drain on kitchen paper and keep warm while you cook the remainder of the pakoras. Serve warm with the chutney.

02 MEAT

Ahhhh, the smell of meat cooking. Whether it's being roasted, grilled, barbecued or stewed (the list is endless), for me that smell is up there with freshly baked bread and newly cut grass in spring – the best things in life.

As a Sikh, I don't eat beef, halal or kosher meat because of my religious beliefs, but this has never stopped me cooking with the finest British pork, lamb, chicken and game at home, and as a chef, of course, I've also learned how to cook beef.

I am so grateful to my chef lecturers at Telford College in Edinburgh who taught us how to use the cheaper cuts of the animal before we moved on to the finer cuts. The skills needed to coax out flavour, taste and tenderness from the cheaper cuts teach you to respect the finer cuts and cook them correctly.

In this chapter I have used a medley of cooking techniques and flavourings. I have mainly gone for cheap cuts, and some recipes deliberately have a wee bit left over so that the extra can be used in other recipes in the book – all of which will help you keep an eye on the purse strings!

Beef brisket in beer with parsley potatoes

This is a real winter rib-sticker. Brisket is a lovely cheap cut from behind the ribs and here it is cooked very slowly until the meat falls apart, then it's snuggled up with lovely, fluffy tatties to soak up that wonderful gravy. Make sure you buy a nice thick, even piece of beef so it all cooks at the same rate and you don't get any dry thinner ends. I've gone for Holy Cow Scottish pale ale, which is a favourite of mine, from a local Borders brewery. Its flavour is deliciously malty but just go with a brown ale of your choosing if you can't get hold of it – India Pale Ale works well too.

Serves 4

1kg beef brisket, with a good 2.5cm
   or more of fat on top
4 tbsp rapeseed oil
2 onions, roughly chopped
2 carrots, roughly chopped
2 x 500ml can Holy Cow Scottish ale
   or India Pale Ale
1 litre beef stock
Spiced Pickled Onions
   (see page 251), to serve
Harissa (see page 120), to serve
lemon wedges, to serve

Brisket seasoning
2 tbsp Maldon salt
6 tbsp fresh thyme leaves
   (lots of work but well worth it)
2 bay leaves, crumbled
16 garlic cloves, peeled and crushed
2 tsp crushed chilli flakes
1½ tbsp cracked black pepper

Parsley potatoes
500g pink fir apple potatoes, halved
150g unsalted butter
25g curly parsley, chopped
salt and pepper

1 Remove the brisket from the refrigerator 2 hours before cooking .

2 Combine all the brisket seasoning ingredients in a food processor and rub all over the brisket.

3 Place a large roasting tin over two burners on a high heat for 2 minutes. Add the oil and wait for 30 seconds. Place the seasoned brisket, fat-side down, in the hot oil and seal on both sides until deep brown – about 10 minutes each side.

4 Preheat the oven to 160°C/gas 3. Remove the brisket from the tin and reduce the heat to medium. Add the vegetables to the tin and cook until caramelised – about 3–5 minutes. Stir often with a wooden spoon, scraping up all the crusty bits, then add the ale and bubble to reduce by half. Next add the stock and bring to the boil. Pop in the brisket and switch off the heat. Put a sheet of greaseproof paper and a double layer of foil over the tin, seal well around the edges and place in the oven for 2½ hours.

5 Take the brisket out and check a knife will slide into it like butter – if not, return it to the oven and check the meat at 15-minute intervals.

6 When the beef is ready, take it out of the roasting tin and pop on a baking tray that fits under your grill. Grill the brisket until the top is crispy, then let the meat rest for 10 minutes.

7 Meanwhile, place the potatoes in a pan, cover with cold water, add salt and bring to the boil. Turn the heat down to a simmer and cook the potatoes until they slip off the tip of a knife. Drain and pop back into the pan with the butter and parsley. Season with salt and pepper, pop on the lid, and shake until they start to break up. If you don't have a lid for the pan just lightly crush them with a fork.

8 Slice the meat and serve with the braising liquor and vegetables, parsley potatoes and spiced pickled onions, harissa and wedges of lemon on the side.

Treacle and tamarind glazed beef with fried onions and boiled potatoes

There's a medley of flavours and influences going on here: sweet treacle offsets the sharp, sour, taste of the tamarind. This makes it sound a bit fancy and exotic but that's what I love about it. It's basically an earthy, simple hearty dish – just steak, fried onions and boiled potatoes – that has been given a bit of glamour by some ingredients I always have in my cupboard.

Serves 4

4 x 225g rump steaks with a nice bit
   of top fat
chopped parsley, to garnish

Glaze
200ml water
150g fresh ginger, roughly chopped
   with skin on
200g treacle
100g tamarind paste (if it's very sour
   use less)
10 garlic cloves, bashed
½ tsp chilli flakes

Onions
1 tbsp rapeseed oil
4 red onions, peeled, each cut into
   8 wedges
50g unsalted butter
30g thyme
20g chives, chopped
salt and pepper

1 Place all the glaze ingredients in a pan, bring to the boil and simmer for 10 minutes. Strain through a fine sieve onto a large tray to cool it down as quickly as possible. Transfer to a non-reactive container (stainless steel or glass) that will fit in the fridge. Pop the steaks in the glaze and marinade for 4 hours.

2 For the onions, place the oil in a heavy-bottomed pan over a high heat and bring to a smoking heat. Carefully add the onions (watch you don't get splashed by the spitting fat), then add the butter and thyme. Turn down the heat and cook slowly with a lid on for 20 minutes. Season.

3 Place the potatoes in a pan of cold water, add salt, then cover and bring to the boil. Turn the heat down to a simmer and cook the potatoes until they are done – they should slip off the tip of a knife. Drain, pop back into the pan with the parsley and season with salt and pepper.

Potatoes
700g Charlotte potatoes, peeled
25g curly parsley, chopped

Mustard mayo
200g mayonnaise
2–3 tbsp Dijon mustard
squeeze of lemon juice

4 To make the mustard mayo, simply mix the ingredients together, adding more lemon juice, if necessary, to balance the flavour. Set aside until ready to use.

5 Remove the steaks from the marinade and pat dry. Pour the marinade into a pan, bring to the boil and reduce by half, until a syrup consistency.

6 Heat a griddle, frying pan, or even a barbecue until hot. Cook the steaks (you'll probably need to do them in batches) until they are a nice colour on one side (about 3 minutes), then flip over and cook the other side. Brush the browned side with the reduced glaze. When they are done, take them out of the pan, brush the other side of the steaks with the glaze and let them rest on a plate, covered with foil, for 5 minutes.

7 Place each glazed steak on a plate with a pile of onions and some potatoes. Garnish with the parsley, and serve with the mustard mayo and a drizzle of the glaze.

Galloway shorthorn beef burger with horseradish mayo

Being a Sikh, I don't eat beef and I was always annoyed as a kid that we couldn't have those massive burgers that all our friends were eating. I've always known what to look for when buying beef though. All the great chefs I've worked for have shown me how to get the best quality – look for the grain and the marbling of the fat. Galloway shorthorn beef is some of the best in the world and this burger recipe, thanks to my good friend Cyrus Todiwala, is fabulous. You can buy horseradish sauce and it's great with beef and roasts but I find that it is too punchy and masks a lot of the flavour of the meat so here I have made a sauce that is a bit milder.

Serves 4–6, depending on the size you like them

Burgers

2 tsp black peppercorns (optional)
800g best minced steak (I use Galloway shorthorn)
2 red onions, grated and squeezed out in a tea towel
10 garlic cloves, crushed to a purée
4 tarragon sprigs, chopped
salt,
rapeseed oil, for brushing the burgers

Horseradish mayo

200g mayo
8 tsp freshly grated horseradish (depending on taste you may want it stronger so add more)
salt and pepper
caster sugar, to taste
1 lemon

1 For the mayo, place the mayo and horseradish in a blender and pulse briefly to combine. Season with salt, pepper, sugar and a squeeze of lemon juice, if necessary.

2 If you're using them, start by dry-roasting the black peppercorns in a pan for 5 minutes, then grind them in a spice grinder or pestle and mortar. You don't need to include peppercorns, but they add so much depth to the flavour of the burger.

3 Add all the remaining burger ingredients (except the oil) and mix well then shape into four or six burgers, depending on how big you like them. Pop in the fridge to firm up for as long as possible – at least 1 hour .

4 When you are ready to cook them, heat a large frying pan or griddle until very hot. Brush the burgers with the oil. Grill the burgers until golden brown and slightly charred on one side – about 3–5 minutes, then flip them over. Cook until golden brown and slightly charred on the second side (about 4 minutes for medium–rare) or until cooked to your desired degree of loveliness. Serve with the horseradish mayo and your other burger necessaries.

Cow pie

Growing up, I loved reading *The Beano* and *The Dandy*, so I'm blaming this pie on *The Dandy* character Desperate Dan. Dan's favourite food was 'cow pie', an enormous meat pie with horns sticking out of the top. Sadly *The Dandy* is no longer in print, so this is my homage to Dan.

Serves 6–8

1½ bottles red wine
splash of rapeseed oil
4 small red onions, cut into 2cm dice
6 garlic cloves, crushed
2 carrots, diced
250g button mushrooms, cut into quarters
1kg Scotch silverside beef, cut into 2cm cubes
25g thyme sprigs, tied together with string
4 star anise
salt and pepper
3 tbsp plain flour
a little beef stock (optional)
500g puff pastry
1 egg, beaten

1   Preheat the oven to 190°C/gas 5.

2   Place the wine in a saucepan over a high heat and bubble until you have reduced it by two thirds and are left with 400ml of syrupy red wine. Remove and set aside.

3   Cover the bottom of a casserole with a film of oil and place on a medium–high heat. Add the onions and fry until lightly coloured. Add the garlic, carrots and mushrooms and mix everything together. Stir in the beef, thyme, star anise and a pinch of salt and pepper. Fry for 3–4 minutes, then pour in the reduced wine. Stir in the flour, making sure you do not have any lumps. The meat and everything else should be just covered with the liquid; if not, top up with some beef stock or water. Bring to a simmer, cover the pan with a lid and cook in the oven for about 2½ hours. Check and stir every 30 minutes.

4   When the meat is very tender and the stew is rich, dark and thick, remove it from the oven and leave it to cool down. Leave the oven on. Check the seasoning and take out the star anise and thyme. Pop the stew into a 24cm-diameter pie dish.

5   Roll out the pastry on a floured work surface until about 5mm thick. Moisten the edges of the pie dish with a little beaten egg, then drape the pastry over the dish. Trim off any overhanging pastry using a sharp knife, then press down the edges. Use some of the pastry trimmings to make little curved horns to stick in the pie once cooked. Poke two small holes in the pastry, which will let out the steam as it cooks so that the pastry doesn't become soggy (they'll be covered by the horns later).

6   Brush the pastry with the beaten egg and pop it on the bottom shelf of the oven for 45 minutes or until the pastry is cooked, puffed and golden. Pop the horns on a baking sheet and bake them for the last 10 minutes of the cooking time.

7   When the pie is ready, stick the horns into the holes then serve immediately.

Scotch broth, turnips and kale

This is how I like to have my Scotch broth – big, hearty and chunky, more like a stew – but if you want, you can trim it down and make it more gentle, in which case use some nice diced lamb instead of the lamb neck.

Serves 8

2kg lamb neck steaks, cut through the
  bone into 3cm slices (ask your
  butcher to do this)
2 litres lamb or chicken stock
150g pearl barley, washed in cold
  water until it runs clear
2 celery sticks, trimmed
  and finely chopped
3 small onions, quartered
6 garlic cloves, crushed
6 bay leaves
100g fresh thyme sprigs, tied in a
  bunch with string
4 carrots, cut into 5cm pieces
2 turnips, cut into 5cm cubes
6 small peeled Desiree potatoes,
  each cut into 8
500g kale, picked off the stalk
  and chopped roughly
120g curly parsley, chopped
buttered brown bread, to serve
salt and pepper

1. Heat a large casserole until hot. Season the lamb steaks and fry them until they take on a nice golden colour – you may need to do this in batches. Transfer to a plate or tray.

2. Pour the stock into the hot pan and use a wooden spoon to scrape the bottom so that all the lovely tasty bits come off.

3. Add the lamb back to the pan along with all the lovely juices that have collected on the plate. Bring the stock to the boil, then turn down to a simmer and skim the surface to remove any scum. Add the barley, celery, onions, garlic, bay leaves and thyme bundle, then bring back to the boil and simmer for 1½ hours.

4. Add the carrot, turnip and potatoes and cook on a simmer until the potatoes are just done. Add the kale, bring to a simmer and cook for another 15 minutes. Season, add the chopped parsley and serve with buttered brown bread.

The McTSingh chilli dog

Like I've said, being a Sikh I can't eat beef, so while the Frankfurter sausages in a hot dog are fine, the classic American way of serving a 'chilli dog' – with a spicy beef chilli ladled on top – is out. So when I learned how to be a chef I decided to put my own spin on the concept using pork mince. Depending on how heavy-handed you are with dolloping on your chilli, you might have some left over that you can freeze and use to serve on top of jacket potatoes or in taco shells.

Serves 4

Ginger-garlic-chilli paste
1 tsp cumin seeds
1 tbsp coriander seeds
10cm piece fresh ginger, peeled
   and sliced
8 garlic cloves, peeled and chopped
4 green Serrano chillies, seeds in or
   out, depending on how hot you like
   things (I am an all-in, all-spicy type)

Chilli mince
3 tbsp rapeseed oil
7cm cinnamon stick
4 cloves
3 red onions, finely chopped
1 tsp red chilli powder
½ tsp ground turmeric
2 tbsp tomato purée
500g lean minced pork
3 tomatoes, chopped
2 dried chillies
200ml boiling water
3 tbsp chopped coriander
½ tsp salt

To serve
4 soft sweet hot dog rolls
Dill Pickle and Onions (see page 236)
4 hot dogs (go for jumbo size)
Easy Squeezy Cheese Sauce
   (see page 242)
Chilli Sauce (see page 250)

1 For the ginger-garlic-chilli paste, heat a small frying pan over a medium heat and dry-fry the cumin and coriander seeds for about 1 minute, until toasted and fragrant, then leave to cool.

2 Grind the toasted seeds in a spice grinder or with a pestle and mortar then tip into a food processor or blender with the remaining paste ingredients and a splash of water, and blend to a paste.

3 In a heavy-bottomed pan heat the oil over a medium heat and fry the cinnamon and cloves for 1–2 minutes until fragrant. Add the chopped onion and fry for 10 minutes until softened and browned.

4 Add the chilli powder, turmeric and ginger-garlic-chilli paste, and cook for 3–4 minutes until the mix is golden and fragrant (add a splash of water if it starts to stick to the pan). Add the tomato purée and cook for 1–2 minutes, then add the pork. Stir well to break up any lumps and cook for 5 minutes, stirring often. Add a splash of water if the mixture starts to stick to the pan.

5 Add the tomatoes, dried chillies and boiling water. Stir to mix and simmer for 10 minutes until the liquid has reduced to a rich sauce, then stir through the coriander.

6 To serve, slit the rolls open, warm them and add some of the dill pickle and onions. Pop in a hot dog and then spoon the chilli mince on top. Add the cheese and chilli sauces.

Foxy blonde braised lamb belly with charred onion

Scottish Foxy Blonde pale ale has a great citrussy flavour and aroma that works so well with a nice fatty lamb belly. The charred onion mash was a new one on me – my friend James Hardy showed me how to do it – but that little bit of bitterness as well as sweetness from the burnt onion works so well with the juicy, fatty lamb, braised in the ale.

Serves 4

1.5kg boneless lamb belly, trimmed
good splash of oil
6 red onions, peeled, each cut into
   6 wedges
2 carrots, peeled and chopped
1 large leek, chopped
1 garlic bulb, sliced horizontally though
   the middle
4 rosemary sprigs
600ml hot chicken or vegetable stock
   (or seasoned water if you're stuck)
600ml Foxy Blonde pale ale (or pale
   ale of your choice, preferably with
   citrus notes)

Spice mix

2 tbsp ground coriander
2 tbsp ground cumin
1 tsp ground Szechuan peppercorns
25g thyme leaves, chopped
25g rosemary leaves, chopped
2 tbsp garlic purée
2 tbsp pickled ginger, chopped
1 tsp freshly ground black pepper
1 tsp salt

1 Preheat the oven to 180°C/gas 4.

2 Prepare the spice mix by stirring together the coriander, cumin and ground Szechuan peppercorns in a small pan. Toast the spices over a low heat until fragrant – about 2 minutes. Remove from the heat and transfer to a small mixing bowl. Add the garlic, ginger, chopped herbs, pepper and salt and mix to form a paste.

3 Rub the paste on the inside of the lamb, then transfer to a flat dish. Refrigerate the lamb overnight if possible, or for a couple of hours if not.

4 While the lamb is marinating, start the mash. Pierce the potatoes with a sharp knife in a few places. Bake for 1–1½ hours or until tender. When done, leave to cool slightly then halve each one and scoop out the flesh. Turn the oven down to 150°C/gas 2.

5 Remove the belly from the fridge and roll it up with the spice mixture on the inside – like a meaty Swiss roll – then tie along the joint.

6 Heat a large lidded casserole that will fit in the oven for about 5 minutes, then add a good splash of oil. Add the lamb and fry over a medium heat for 1–2 minutes on all sides or until golden-brown all over. Season the lamb well, then remove from the pan and place on a plate.

7 In the same pan, add the onions and fry until golden brown all over. Take out a quarter of the onions, turn up the heat and keep moving the onions until they start to char. Take out half of the remaining onions and set aside with the golden brown ones then add the carrot, leek and garlic to the pan.

Note
You're going to need some butcher's or kitchen string for this one.

Mash

1kg floury potatoes (King Edward,
   Maris Piper, Wilja, Ailsa or Golden
   Wonder are the ones you want)
75g butter
75–100ml double cream
1 tbsp chopped chives

Crispy greens

30ml sesame oil
800g spring greens, washed, stalks
   removed, leaves shredded
dark soy sauce, to taste

A cheffy tip

If you want, when the lamb
comes out of the oven,
you can leave it to cool
completely in its stock
(preferably overnight).
This lets the lamb firm up so
that when you cut the cold
lamb you get perfect, neat
slices. Heat the sliced lamb
through in the stock then
in the oven, as above, and
make the accompaniments
fresh on the day you're
serving the dish.

8 Place the browned lamb on top of the vegetables, add the rosemary
sprigs and pour over the stock and pale ale to cover the lamb. Cover
with the lid and place into the oven to braise for 3–4 hours, or until the
lamb is very tender. (Leave the oven on.)

9 Remove the lamb from the pot, transfer to a warm plate and cover
with foil.

10 Pass the stock from the lamb pan through a sieve into a clean pan
and bubble over a high heat. Bubble until the liquid has reduced by
half, seasoning to taste.

11 Meanwhile, finish the mash. Mash the potato flesh well, either with
a ricer or just with a fork, until it is as fine as you can make it. Transfer
to a clean pan over a low heat, add the butter and cream and blend well to
the right consistency. Stir in the reserved charred onions and the chopped
chives and heat until piping hot.

12 To make the crispy greens, heat a wok until very hot. Add the sesame
oil and roll over the inside of the wok. Add the spring greens – they
will spit so be careful. Toss the greens with a pair of tongs or move them
about with a wooden spoon till the wok stops shouting, then add soy sauce
to taste while continuing to toss the greens. When they are ready to serve,
they will be bright green and still crispy – this should take only about 3
minutes in total.

13 To serve, slice the lamb and place in a serving dish. Pour over some
of the reduced stock and pop into the oven to make sure it is nice
and hot. Scoop the mash on to plates, place the greens to the side and pop
on some lamb slices, then spoon over more of the sauce.

Chipotle lamb meatballs with baked rice and avocado cream

I always say a little bit of spice is nice, and here lovely lamb mince is lifted with smoky chipotle chillies and cumin. Chipotle chillies are a variety of Mexican chilli that have been smoked and dried. They have quite a mild heat and give dishes a warm earthy flavour rather than a kick. If you prefer, you can just grill or pan-fry the meatballs and serve them with whichever sauce you fancy from the Pandora's Box chapter – the Tomato Salsa (see page 244) works well, as does Chermoula (see page 52).

Serves 4

Meatballs
2 tsp coriander seeds
3 tsp cumin seeds
5cm whole dried chipotle chilli or 2 tsp ground chipotle chillies
675g minced lamb shoulder
2 small potatoes, peeled, boiled and grated
100g onion, finely chopped
7 garlic cloves, crushed
2.5cm piece fresh ginger, peeled and minced
20g fresh coriander, chopped
1 tsp sea salt
2 tbsp rapeseed oil

Sauce
450g green tomatoes (if you can't get them, use unripe, bullet-hard tomatoes)
4 chipotle chillies in vinegar
100g coriander leaves
50ml sherry vinegar
salt and pepper
2 tbsp rapeseed oil
600ml chicken stock (fresh is best, but if you're stuck use a cube or powder)

1 First make the meatballs. Dry-fry the coriander and cumin seeds in a small pan over a low heat until fragrant and golden in colour – about 4–6 minutes. Leave to cool.

2 Place the whole chilli, if using, in a dry frying pan over a medium and toast until the chilli begins to puff up. Take it out of the pan, cut it in half, then remove the seeds and stem and discard. Place the chilli (or ground chipotle chillies, if using) in a spice mill or pestle and mortar. Add the toasted seeds and grind until fine.

3 Transfer this spice mixture to a large bowl along with the minced lamb, potatoes, onion, garlic, ginger, coriander, salt and oil. Mix with your hands until well combined. Form into balls about the size of a golf ball, then pop them into the fridge for an hour to firm up.

4 To make the sauce, cut the green tomatoes in half and pop them into a blender. Add the chipotle chillies, coriander and vinegar and purée until smooth. Season to taste with salt and pepper.

5 Heat the oil in a heavy-bottomed pan over a medium–high heat. Add the green tomato purée and fry until thickened – about 6–7 minutes. Make sure you keep stirring, as the mixture will stick to the pan. Carefully add the stock and bring to a boil. Reduce the heat to a simmer, add the meatballs, bring back to a simmer and cook until the meatballs are cooked through and the sauce has thickened – about 20–25 minutes.

Baked rice

2 tbsp rapeseed oil
2.5cm piece cinnamon stick
2 cloves
8 black peppercorns
1 large Spanish onion, finely chopped
2 green chillies, deseeded and chopped
2.5cm piece fresh ginger, grated
1 bay leaf
200g basmati rice
100g frozen petit pois
salt

Avocado cream

2 ripe Hass avocados
juice of 2 limes
1 tsp chopped coriander leaves
salt
Tabasco sauce, to taste

6 Meanwhile, make the baked rice. Preheat the oven to 150°C/gas 2. Heat the oil over a medium heat in a large heavy-bottomed pan that has a tight-fitting lid and can fit in the oven. (If you don't have a lid, you can use tin foil to make a nice tight cover for the rice.) Add the cinnamon, cloves and peppercorns and fry until fragrant. Now add the onion, green chillies, ginger and bay leaf and fry until the onions are transparent (not brown). Add the rice, petits pois, salt and just enough water to cover the rice. Mix well and bring to the boil over a high heat.

7 Take the pan off the heat, pop on the lid and put in the oven for 20 minutes or until the rice is cooked and the water has evaporated.

8 To make the avocado cream, scoop the avocado flesh into a blender, add the other ingredients and purée until smooth. Serve the meatballs with the baked rice and avocado cream.

Lamb masala kebabs with salted cucumber and coconut chutney

Masala – funny how we now take this word for granted! I can remember putting this on a Sunday lunch menu with the blessing of the sous-chef, as the head chef was off every Sunday. The first order came and when it went out it was promptly sent back as 'funny food' – the gent who had ordered it was expecting Marsala wine! This recipe is a great way of getting you into marinating meat, the idea being that natural yoghurt or anything acidic in your marinade tenderises the meat and pushes the flavour into it.

Serves 4–6

1 tsp coriander seeds
1 tsp cumin seeds
seeds of 2 large black cardamom pods
   (if you can't get black pods use 4
   green; they will be sweeter and you
   won't get a smokiness but they will
   still taste good)
2.5cm piece cinnamon stick
3 cloves
10 black peppercorns
50g fresh ginger, peeled and
   roughly chopped
6 garlic cloves, peeled
1 large Spanish onion, roughly
   chopped
1 tsp chilli powder
½ tsp turmeric powder
2 bay leaves
1 tsp salt
250g natural yoghurt
juice of 1 lemon
white distilled vinegar (optional)
500g lamb neck fillet, cut into
   bite-sized cubes

1 Gently toast the coriander, cumin, cardamom, cinnamon, cloves and black peppercorns in a pan over a low heat for about 5 – 8 minutes till they are aromatic. Allow to cool, then grind to a powder.

2 Pop this spice powder into a food processor with all the remaining ingredients (except the vinegar and meat) and blend to a paste. If it is too thick and not blending, add a touch of vinegar to it.

3 In a non-reactive bowl (glass or stainless steel), mix the paste with the meat and marinate in the fridge for at least 4 – 5 hours, or overnight if possible. This will give the meat time to take on all the wonderful flavours but most of all let the acid and the enzymes in the yoghurt tenderise the meat.

Salted cucumber and coconut chutney

1 cucumber, peeled, deseeded and cut
    into roughly 1cm cubes
1 coconut, peeled and cut into cubes
3 tbsp rapeseed oil
1 tsp black peppercorns
2 dried red chillies
½ tsp mustard seeds
1 mango, as ripe as possible, peeled
    and flesh grated to the stone
juice of 1–2 limes
salt

4   To make the chutney, put the cucumber into a colander and sprinkle with salt. Toss to make sure it is well seasoned and leave to drain for 1 hour, then rinse in lots of cold water and leave to drain again.

5   Put the coconut pieces into a food processor. Whizz to get a finely grated coconut mixture.

6   Heat the oil in a heavy-based pan. When hot, add the black peppercorns and fry for a few seconds, then add the chillies and mustard seeds and fry till they start to pop. Take off the heat.

7   Place the coconut in a bowl and add the cucumber, mango, juice of 1 lime and ½ teaspoon salt, stir in the spices and mix well. Check the seasoning, adding more salt and lime if necessary.

8   Preheat the oven to 240°C/gas 9 or prepare your barbecue.

9   Pop about 125g worth of meat either on one large skewer or on to a couple of small ones. I prefer to use metal skewers as the heat gets right to the centre of the meat quicker but if you use wooden skewers make sure you soak them in water for 1 hour first to prevent them burning. Roast in the oven or cook on the barbecue for 15–20 minutes or until nice and brown. Serve the kebabs with the chutney.

Pictured overleaf

Scrumpets

I came across scrumpets on a boys' night out down in Newcastle. We were away
to see the Toon Army play, and I admit, a few bottles of Newcastle Brown Ale later
I was happy to get scrumpets placed in front of me. They're a traditional, salty,
meaty bar snack to soak up your ale – wonderful!

**Serves 8–10
as a starter or snack**

2 tbsp ground coriander
2 tbsp ground cumin
1 tsp ground Szechuan peppercorns
1 tsp freshly ground black pepper
2 tbsp garlic purée
2 tbsp chopped fresh ginger
2 tsp chopped thyme leaves
1 tsp chopped rosemary leaves
1kg boneless lamb belly, trimmed
3 red onions, sliced
2 carrots, sliced
1 leek, sliced
1 garlic bulb , cut in half horizontally
4 rosemary sprigs
150ml chicken or vegetable stock
200ml milk
2 eggs
1 tsp English mustard
250g breadcrumbs
200g flour
salt and pepper
oil, for frying
lemon wedges, to serve
Chippy Sauce with a Kick (see page
    241), to serve
Chermoula (see page 52), to serve

Note
You'll need to start
preparing this well in
advance – at least a day
before you want to serve it
but ideally two.

1   Combine the coriander, cumin and Szechuan and black peppercorns
    in a small pan. Toast over a low heat until fragrant – about 2 minutes.
Remove from the heat and transfer the spices to a small mixing bowl. Add
the garlic purée, ginger, chopped thyme and rosemary leaves and salt, and
mix to form a paste. Rub the paste on the lamb and refrigerate for at least
2 hours, or overnight if possible.

2   Preheat the oven to 150°C/gas 2.

3   Place the onions, carrot, leek, garlic and rosemary in an ovenproof dish
    that has a tight-fitting lid. Put the lamb on top and pour in the stock.
Cover with the lid or a double layer of greaseproof paper and tin foil. Cook
in the oven for about 2–3 hours or until the lamb is very tender, basting
regularly – you may need to turn the oven down a little during cooking.
Leave to cool down overnight.

4   Scrape away any cooking fat residue from the meat and any surplus
    fat that hasn't rendered down during cooking. Cut the meat into strips
roughly 1 x 3–4cm.

5   Mix the milk, eggs and mustard together in a shallow bowl. Put the
    breadcrumbs and flour in two separate shallow bowls and season
the flour.

6   Dip the lamb pieces in the flour, shake off the excess, then dip them
    in the beaten egg and finally coat in the breadcrumbs. Shake off the
excess and lay them on a tray.

7   Put a deep-fat fryer on to 180°C or fill a deep pan a quarter full with
    oil and heat. Deep-fry in batches of about 8–10 for 3–4 minutes, until
golden brown. Remove with a slotted spoon and drain on kitchen paper.
Keep the cooked scrumpets warm in a low oven until they are all cooked.
Serve with lemon wedges and the sauces.

Cabbage and ribs

Cabbage and ribs: a dish but also the nickname of my football team, Hibs (Hibernian), or the famous Hibbies. This is my Gran's recipe that I always get her to cook for me, and it's her way of making simple things – chopped white cabbage and bashed lamb ribs – go far and taste wonderful. There's not much meat on the lamb ribs, but the fat that renders out of them makes this taste divine.

Serves 4

1½ tbsp rapeseed oil
2 small Spanish onions, chopped
2 tsp crushed garlic
100ml water
1½ tsp turmeric
2½ tsp garam masala
½ tsp red chilli powder
400g tin chopped tomatoes
5cm piece fresh ginger, chopped
1 tsp crushed green chillies
salt
500g lamb ribs (cut in half – ask your
   butcher to do this for you, unless you
   own a large cleaver)
½ white cabbage, sliced
1 tbsp chopped coriander, to serve

1 Heat the oil in a casserole with a lid and fry the onions over a medium heat until golden brown. Add the garlic and cook for another minute, then pour in the water, followed by all the dry spices and stir. Bring to the boil, then add the tomatoes, ginger, green chillies and salt and bring back to the boil.

2 Add the ribs and coat in the sauce. Add the cabbage and cover with a tight-fitting lid. Slowly cook for about 2 hours, stirring from time to time, until the meat falls off the bone and the cabbage is cooked in its own juices. Sprinkle with chopped coriander to serve.

Roast pork belly with chermoula

I love pork belly but in this dish the chermoula is the star. Get a nice crispy pork belly, add chermoula and it's a show-stopping dish. The potent North African spicy sauce is like a punchy salsa verde with a spicy kick. A dollop of this will transform any piece of grilled fish or roast meat.

Serves 6

1.5kg boneless pork belly, with rind
4 tsp black peppercorns
1½ tbsp sea salt

Chermoula
100g coriander
50g flat-leaf parsley leaves
10 garlic cloves
2 tsp cumin seeds, toasted until they change colour, then ground
1 tsp smoked paprika
1 green Serrano chilli
¼ tsp dried chilli flakes
100ml rapeseed oil
zest and juice of 2 lemons
½ tsp salt

1. Pop all the ingredients for the chermoula into a blender and whizz until you have a rough purée. Add more oil if it is too thick then check the seasoning. If you do any left over, the chermoula keeps well in the fridge up to 1 week, though you need to cover it with a layer of oil. It's normal for it to discolour slightly.

2. Score the pork rind with a knife at 5mm intervals. Pat it thoroughly dry with kitchen paper then leave for 2 hours until completely dried out. It needs to be really dry so that you get crunchy crackling.

3. Toast the peppercorns in a dry pan until they smell aromatic. Cool and grind in a pepper mill or mortar and pestle and mix with the salt.

4. Pat the pork flesh completely dry with kitchen paper. Rub the salt and pepper mixture all over the flesh, but not the rind. Leave for at least 1 hour, or as long as possible, to allow the flavours to permeate. When you're ready to roast the pork, preheat the oven to 230°C/gas 8.

5. Place the pork on a rack sitting above a roasting tray. Roast for 30 minutes, then reduce the heat to 160°C/gas 3 and roast for a further 1½ hours. The meat should be meltingly soft and will pull away easily if you try and pinch a piece. Remove from the oven and allow to rest for 10 minutes, loosely covered with a piece of tin foil to keep it warm.

6. To serve, hack off some crackling, slice the meat and serve with a dollop of chermoula.

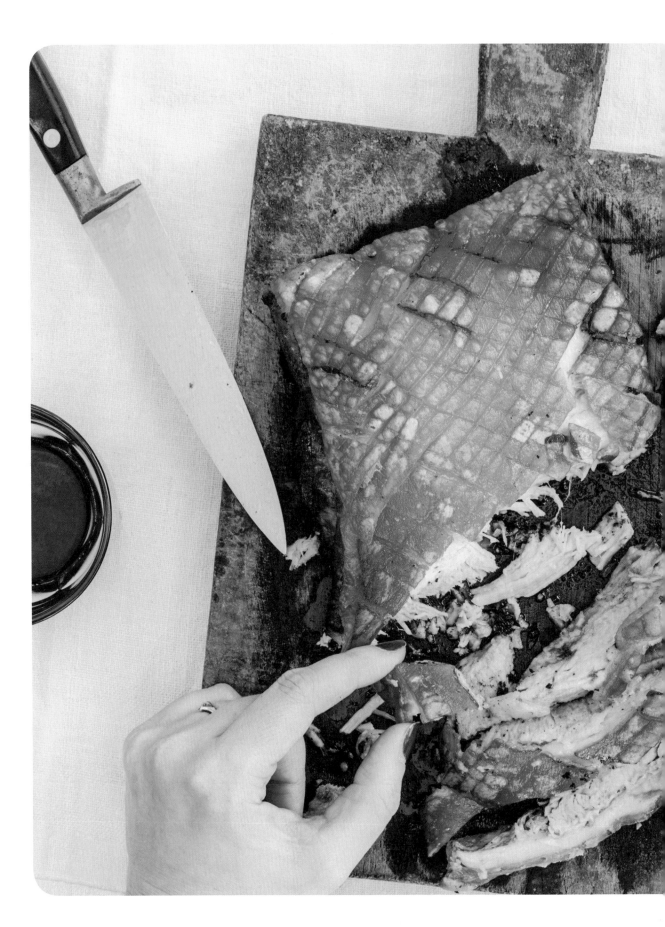

Baked sausages with apples, mushroom and beer gravy

This is a 'toad-in-the-hole' of epic flavour. When I was growing up, my mum used to make this for tea but it was never called 'toad-in-the-hole'. So when I was having tea at a friend's house one afternoon, I was so excited when he told me we were having this exotic- and weird-sounding dish called 'toad-in-the-hole'. How deflated was I when it was just baked sausages... When I got home I had words with my mum, asking her to explain why it wasn't called that in our family. The only explanation I got was that the name made her squeamish – as if we would ever have had toads in the house!

Serves 6

rapeseed oil
50g butter
8 large good-quality pork sausages
8 fresh thyme sprigs
2 Russet apples, peeled cored and cut
  into chunks
1 Bramley apple, peeled, cored and
  cut into chunks half the size of the
  Russet ones
2 tbsp chopped parsley, to garnish

Batter
3 eggs
280ml full-fat milk
100g plain flour, sifted
pinch of salt

Gravy
splash of vegetable oil
3 garlic cloves, peeled and crushed
250g Spanish onions, peeled and sliced
salt and pepper
1 tbsp treacle
3 tbsp Worcestershire sauce
600ml ale of your choice (I would
  use Eighty Shilling or any good
  brown ale)
600ml strong chicken stock, or
  chicken stock cube(s) dissolved in
  600ml water
4–6 large portabello mushrooms,
  sliced
1½ tsp cornflour mixed with 3 tbsp
  cold water

1 Preheat the oven to 200°C/gas 6. Mix the batter ingredients together and put in the fridge.

2 Pour 1cm rapeseed oil into a 20 x 25cm baking tin, then place this on the middle shelf of your oven. Place tin foil on the shelf below to catch any oil or batter that come over the top.

3 Put a splash of oil in a heavy-based frying pan and when it is hot add the butter and brown the sausages all over then take them out of the pan. Take the tin out of the oven – the oil should be smoking – and place your sausages, thyme and apple in it. Carefully pour over the batter; it will bubble and possibly even spit a little, so be careful. Gently put the tin back in the oven and bake for 25–30 minutes. Don't open the door for at least 20 minutes, so as not to ruin the batter – it can be a bit temperamental when rising. Remove from the oven when golden and crisp.

4 For the gravy, heat a film of oil in a heavy-based pan and fry the garlic and onion till soft. Add salt and pepper and turn up the heat. As soon as the onions take on some colour, add the treacle and Worcestershire and cook for 5 minutes, stirring all the time. Add the beer and bubble until reduced to a syrup, then add the stock, bring to the boil and add the mushrooms. Reduce to a simmer and reduce by half then stir in the cornflour mixture and bring to boil. Season and serve with the sausages.

Banh mi (well, my take on it)

The key to this filled Vietnamese baguette is flavour, flavour, flavour.
You take any filling base you want – pork, fish, prawns, tofu – whatever you've got,
then load it up with your secret weapon, one of the amazing Vietnamese sauces
below, to create a sandwich like no other.

Serves 4

Sandwich stuff

1 thin baguette or 4 mini baguettes
6 spring onions, shredded
2 carrots, shredded
1 cucumber, cut into thin strips
½ bunch coriander, stalks removed
mayonnaise
fun stuff: you can have whatever meat
   you like (leftover pork shoulder,
   brisket, even the lamb from the
   Scotch broth picked off the bone),
   fish, cheese, tofu…

Nuoc cham dipping sauce

(good with anything)
4 garlic cloves, crushed
2 red bird's eye chillies, chopped
4 tsp brown sugar
juice of 2 limes
4 tbsp nuoc mam (Vietnamese fish
   sauce; if you can't get this use Thai
   fish sauce

Nuoc leo

(a hot peanut dipping sauce, awesome
with all things pork)
1 tbsp vegetable oil
2 red bird's eye chillies, chopped
2 garlic cloves, crushed
115g unsalted roasted peanuts,
   finely chopped
150ml chicken stock
60ml coconut milk
15ml hoisin suce
15ml nuoc mam (see above)
1 tbsp brown sugar

1. Preheat the oven to 160°C/gas 3.

2. Get your baguette, split it and scoop out the soft white middle (keep this for breadcrumbs, soups etc.). Pop the bread in the hot oven just long enough to crisp it, then remove and let it cool.

3. For the nuoc cham sauce, simply mix all the ingredients together.

4. For the nuoc leo sauce, heat the oil in a wok or frying pan and add the chilli and garlic. Once they start to colour, add half the peanuts. Cook until the nuts release their oil.

5. Add the rest of the ingredients except the remaining peanuts, bring to the boil and simmer for 5–10 minutes. Take off the heat, add the rest of the peanuts and serve the sauce hot or cold.

6. Load up your baguette base with all the filling stuff then add copious amounts of your chosen sauce.

Pork shoulder with ginger beer and bok choi

Pork shoulder and ginger beer: sounds a bit weird, but ginger beer – the cloudy, traditionally made, spicy ginger beer – works well with the lovely pork shoulder and its mix of fat and lean meat. This recipe makes a lot and you'll have enough left over to use in the Pulled Pork Buns (see page 66) or make sarnies.

Serves 6–8, with leftovers

Burgers

3kg bone-in pork shoulder, skin on
salt and pepper
2 tbsp rapeseed oil
120g smoked streaky bacon, chopped
3 red onions, thinly sliced
2 cooking apples, peeled, cored and
   quartered
1 garlic bulb, chopped
4 tsp fennel seeds, toasted and ground
4 tsp crushed coriander seeds
150g fresh ginger, washed and sliced
   with skin on
500ml natural-brewed cloudy
   ginger beer
about 1 litre vegetable stock
   (I use Marigold bouillon powder)
Mashed potatoes, to serve (optional)

Bok choi

1 tbsp rapeseed oil
4 bunches bok choi, washed and
   quartered
2 garlic cloves, thinly sliced
1 tbsp honey
2 tbsp soy sauce
¼ tsp sesame oil
100g pickled ginger
100g salted peanuts

1 Preheat the oven to 150°C/gas 2.

2 Season the pork shoulder with salt and pepper. Add the oil to a frying pan and sear the pork, fat-side down, until golden – about 5 minutes. Flip and repeat, then put to one side.

3 In a casserole dish or heavy-based pan that fits in the oven, fry the bacon over a medium–low heat, until the fat is rendered – about 10 minutes. Transfer the bacon to a plate using a slotted spoon – you want to keep the bacon fat in the pan for flavour.

4 Add the onions and apples to the pan and cook over a medium–high heat, stirring occasionally, until caramelised – about 25 minutes.

5 Add the garlic, fennel seeds and coriander seeds to the pan. Cook until fragrant – about 2 minutes. Add the fresh ginger, ginger beer, stock and cooked bacon and bring to a simmer.

6 Return the pork to the pan, then bring to boil. Pop on a tight-fitting lid or use tin foil to make a lid (put a piece of greaseproof paper between the tin foil and the food to stop it breaking down). Transfer to the oven, and cook, basting every hour, until the meat is falling off the bone – about 4 hours.

7 For the bok choi, heat the oil in a large wok over a high heat and swirl to coat. Add the bok choi and stir-fry for 2 minutes, or until just wilted. Add the garlic, honey and soy sauce. Stir-fry for 2–3 minutes or until the bok choi is just tender. Remove from the heat. Toss through the sesame oil, ginger and peanuts.

8 When the pork is ready, lift it out of the pan and pass the cooking liquid through a sieve. Pour the strained sauce over the meat and serve with bok choi and some mash.

Kinky sausage rolls

These are sausage rolls, adult style. They're huge – these are meals not snacks – and as sausage meat is such a great carrier for all sorts of wonderful flavours, I've given you four different options for spicing them up and packing in some punch. Get your sausage meat, have a look at the flavouring options over the page and get experimenting. Whichever you choose, the baking instructions are the same. A word about size: this recipe makes three large sausage rolls and each roll is enough to serve at least six people as a full meal (served with salad and, if you're me, some Desperate Dan Beans, see page 26). Why so much? Well if you're going to go to the hassle of making sausage rolls, you might as well have some left over for next time. The unbaked rolls freeze brilliantly so you've got instant dinner for another day. Simply defrost in the fridge overnight then paint on the egg wash and bake as instructed. If you're not keen on buying quite so much sausage meat in one go, you can halve or quarter the recipe.

Makes 3 huge rolls, enough to serve up to 4 each

800g ready-rolled puff pastry
1.2kg sausage meat
2 eggs, beaten with a splash of milk to make an egg wash
poppy seeds, for sprinkling

1. Preheat the oven to 220°C/gas 7. Line a large baking sheet with baking paper.

2. Place the pastry on to a lightly floured work surface board, split into three portions and roll each out to a rectangle about the size of an A4 sheet of paper (30 x 20cm). They should be about 3mm thick.

3. Mix the sausage meat with your chosen flavouring (see page 62), place a line of sausage mixture down the middle of each pastry rectangle, then brush each with the egg wash on one edge.

4. Fold one side of the pastry over on to the egg-washed side. Press down to seal with a fork and trim any excess. Repeat with the other rectangles.

5. Place the sausage rolls on to a baking tray, brush with egg wash and sprinkle poppy seeds on top.

6. Cook for 30–35 minutes in the oven until the pastry is golden-brown and the sausage is cooked through. Eat warm or cold.

Mushroom and truffle

80g butter
6 shallots, chopped
salt and pepper
100ml white wine
300g wild or button mushrooms, finely chopped
2 tbsp Worcestershire sauce
2½ tbsp chopped thyme leaves
20g tarragon, chopped
3 tsp truffle oil

Melt the butter in a pan, add the shallots, salt and pepper and fry until softened. Add the wine, mushrooms, Worcestershire sauce, thyme and tarragon and cook until there is no liquid left in the pan. Spread out on a large tray to cool.

Put the sausage meat in a big bowl with the cooled mixture and other ingredients. Fry a little bit of the mixture to check the seasoning and adjust as needed. Continue as in the basic recipe.

Fennel and orange

1 fennel bulb, finely chopped
200g shallots
zest and juice of 2 oranges
20g dill, chopped
2 tsp fennel seeds, toasted and roughly crushed
1 tsp chilli flakes
6 garlic cloves, crushed
salt and pepper

Place three quarters of the fennel in a heavy pan with the shallots, orange zest and juice. Bring to the boil then simmer until the fennel is cooked through. Spread out on a tray to cool.

Put the sausage meat in a big bowl with all the other ingredients (including the cooked and raw fennel) and mix well. Fry a little bit of the mixture to check the seasoning and adjust as needed. Continue as in the basic recipe.

Sage and apple

50g butter
40g sage, finely chopped
200g shallots, chopped
2 cooking apples, chopped into 1–2 cm chunks
2 sweet eating apples, peeled and chopped into 1–2 cm chunks
6 garlic cloves, crushed
salt and pepper

Melt the butter in a pan, add the sage and shallots and sweat until cooked. Spread out on a tray to cool.

Put the sausage meat in a big bowl, add the cooled mixture and other ingredients and mix well. Fry a little bit of the mixture to check the seasoning and adjust as needed. Continue as in the basic recipe.

Chilli, cheese and pineapple

200g shallots, chopped
50g unsalted butter
6 garlic cloves, crushed
5 red finger chillies, chopped up with the seeds
400g strong Cheddar, cut into 1cm cubes
1 pineapple, peeled, cored and diced into 2cm pieces
salt and pepper

Fry the shallots with the butter, garlic and chilli. When cooked, spread out on a tray to cool.

Put the sausage meat in a big bowl, add the cooled mixture and other ingredients and mix well. Fry a little bit of the mixture to check the seasoning and adjust as needed. Continue as in the basic recipe.

Chilli pig pie

There are pies and then there are pies, and I reckon this one is pretty special. It's certainly unusual, I'll give it that. Although it's firmly British on the outside, once you crack open the pastry topping and a wonderful, fragrant aroma hits you, there's a little bit of Asia packed inside. Fish sauce, coriander, soy sauce, five-spice and chillies all waft out and I just want to dive straight in. Serve it with some fluffy mash to soak up all that spice and goodness.

Serves 4–6

1 tbsp five-spice powder
1 large Spanish onion, chopped
5 garlic cloves
4 tbsp chopped fresh ginger
1kg boneless, rindless pork belly
150ml soy sauce
100ml sweet sherry
500ml chicken stock

Rest of the filling

2 red peppers, finely shredded
2 bunches spring onions, finely
   shredded
3 tomatoes, deseeded and cut into
   8 petals
15g tarragon, chopped
30g coriander, chopped
juice of 3 limes
3 tbsp Thai sweet chilli sauce
2 tbsp Thai fish sauce
1 bird's eye chilli, chopped (optional
   depending on how chilli-ish you
   want the pie)

Topping

flour, for dusting
500g puff pastry
1 egg, beaten

1 Place the five-spice powder, onion, garlic and ginger in a food processor and process to make a paste.

2 Rub the paste all over the pork and leave overnight if possible, or for at least a couple of hours if not.

3 Preheat the oven to 150°C/gas 2.

4 Pour the soy sauce, sherry and stock into a pan with a tight-fitting lid or a roasting tin and bring to the boil. Add the pork and cover with the lid or with damp greaseproof paper and a double layer of foil if using the tin (it needs to be well sealed so that it can steam. Roast for 2½–3 hours until the meat is very tender when pierced with a fork. Leave the meat to cool to room temperature in the liquid. When cool, cut into bite-sized cubes. Turn the oven up to 200°C/gas 6.

5 Mix the pork with all the filling ingredients and pop into a 24cm-diameter pie dish. Roll out the pastry on a lightly floured work surface until about 5mm thick. Moisten the edges of the pie dish with a little beaten egg, then drape the pastry over the dish. Trim off any overhanging pastry using a sharp knife, then press down the edges. Make a slit or small hole in the centre of the pastry to allow the steam to escape (to prevent the pastry going soggy). Brush with the beaten egg, then bake for about 20–25 minutes, until golden brown.

Pictured overleaf

Pulled pork buns, green papaya, lemongrass and sesame dressing

Well this is where the leftover Pork Shoulder with Ginger Beer (see page 60) comes in! It tastes brilliant in these steamed buns, but don't stop there: you can also use leftover lamb, beef, mince or prawns – the possibilities are endless.

Makes 12–16 buns

Dough

1 x 7g sachet active dried yeast
300ml tepid water
430g plain flour
1 tbsp caster sugar
1 tsp baking powder
2 tbsp diced lard

Filling

1 tbsp toasted sesame oil
3 spring onions, finely chopped
200g leftover pork shoulder (see page 60) or shop-bought roast pork, finely chopped or pulled
3 tbsp hoisin sauce
1 tsp cornflour
1 tbsp water
1 tbsp rice vinegar (but any vinegar will do)
2 tsp chopped coriander

1. To make the dough, mix the yeast and water in a bowl and leave until it becomes foamy – this will take about 10 minutes.

2. Mix the flour, sugar, baking powder and lard in another bowl and make a well in the centre. Pour in the yeast mixture, mix well and knead into a smooth ball. Cover the bowl with cling film, and let sit in a warm place until doubled in size – this will take about 2 hours.

3. Knead the dough until smooth and elastic – about 5 minutes. Shape into 12–16 equal-sized balls.

4. To make the filling, heat the sesame oil in a heavy-based or non-stick pan over a medium–high heat. Add the spring onions and fry for a minute, then add the pork and hoisin sauce and cook for about 3 minutes.

5. Dissolve the cornflour in the water and vinegar in a small cup. Add this to the pork mixture and cook until the sauce thickens – about 1 minute. Remove from the heat and leave to cool before adding the coriander.

6. To fill the buns, place a dough ball in the palm of one hand and, with the thumb of your other hand, make a well in the centre. Fill this with the pork mixture (about 1½ tablespoons of filling) and seal by pinching the dough closed.

7. Place a 5cm-square, lightly oiled piece of greaseproof paper over the pinched area (this will be the bottom of the bun), and pop on a tray. Do the same with the other dough balls, covering the finished balls with a damp cloth as you work. Snip a cross in the top of each bun with a pair of scissors.

8. To steam the buns, use a bamboo, stainless-steel or electric steamer. Place a batch of buns in the steamer, paper-side down, and steam until puffed – about 12 minutes. Repeat with the remaining buns.

Green papaya salad

1 small green papaya peeled,
   deseeded and grated
150g beansprouts
3 spring onions, shredded
20 cherry tomatoes, cut into quarters
100g salted peanuts, chopped
zest of 1 lime (use one of the limes for
   the dressing before you juice it)

Dressing

150g tender centres of lemongrass
   stalks (only the bottom 7–8cm is
   edible when eating raw)
50g coriander, chopped
50g basil leaves, chopped
100g fresh ginger, peeled
1 fresh bird's eye chilli, or more to taste
½ tsp chopped garlic
3 shallots or 1 small red onion
2 tbsp palm or brown sugar, or more
   to taste
2 tsp sesame seeds
1 tbsp toasted sesame seed oil
1 tbsp fish sauce, or more to taste
juice of 3 limes, or more to taste

9   To make the salad dressing, combine all the ingredients in a blender and taste to check the seasoning. Place all the salad ingredients in a bowl and add dressing to taste. Serve the salad with the pork buns and the extra dressing on the side.

Ecky thump

Growing up in the '70s, I loved watching the The Goodies, and this recipe is named after their eponymous comedy sketch. One of the characters reveals himself to be a master of the secret Lancastrian martial art, 'ecky thump', which involves hitting unsuspecting victims with black puddings... There's nothing wrong with a bit of great black pudding, and to make it even more unctuous, put a pig's trotter in with it – the back ones are meatier but front ones will do.

Makes 12 fritters, to serve 4–6

450g Stornaway black pudding
   (or any other good one)
1 small onion, finely chopped
25g butter
1 tbsp flat-leaf parsley, chopped
salt and pepper
200ml milk
2 eggs
1 tsp English mustard
250g panko breadcrumbs
200g flour
oil, for frying
Chunky Piccalilli (see page 230),
   to serve
Aioli (see page 248), to serve

For the trotter
1 pig's trotter
2 onions, peeled and cut in half
2 carrots, peeled and left whole
2 celery sticks, cut in half
2 garlic bulbs,
   cut in half through the equator
8 bay leaves
10 thyme sprigs
10 peppercorns
3 star anise

1. Place the trotter in a large pan, cover with cold water and bring to the boil, then simmer for 5 minutes. Drain off the cooking water and rinse the trotter in cold water.

2. Place the trotter back in the pan, cover with fresh cold water and bring to the boil. Skim off any scum, then add all the other trotter ingredients and turn to a simmer. Continue to cook and skim this stock for about 2½ hours until the trotter has fallen apart. Keep an eye on the pan to make sure it doesn't boil dry and top up with water if necessary.

3. While the trotter is cooking, grate the black pudding into a large bowl, cover with a tea towel and leave to get to room temperature.

4. Fry the onion in the butter until soft, then season, add the parsley and pop onto a plate to cool.

5. When the trotter is cooked, lift the trotter pieces out with a slotted spoon and place on to a tray. Strain the stock into a bowl and keep as a wonderful base for soups, stews and sauces. Pick through the colander or sieve and discard everything apart from any meat or skin off the trotter.

6. Put on a pair of rubber washing-up gloves to work with the trotter while it is hot. If you don't have rubber gloves, let the trotter cool enough for you to handle it. Pick off all the meat, skin and connective tissue from the trotter and chop very finely into 3mm bits. Now mix the trotters with the black pudding and the shallot mixture remembering to add a wee bit of salt and a good grinding of black pepper.

7 Line a large shallow oven tray with cling film. Spread the ecky thump mixture inside and pat it down until 1.5cm thick. Chill for a couple of hours to allow the mixture to firm up to make it easier to cut out. Using a 5cm round cutter, cut out as many circles as you can. Then bring the excess mixture back together and pat down again.

8 Mix the milk, eggs and mustard together in a shallow bowl. Put the breadcrumbs and flour in separate shallow bowls and season the flour. Dip the discs in the flour, shake off any excess, then dip in the beaten egg and finally coat in the breadcrumbs. Shake off the excess and lay them on a tray.

9 Put a deep-fat fryer on to 180°C or fill a deep pan a quarter full with oil and heat. Fry the fritters in batches of 4–6, depending on the size of your pan, for 4 minutes, or until golden. Keep the cooked fritters warm in a low oven while you fry the rest. Serve with the piccalilli and aioli.

Chicken dumplings with apricot and honey sprouts

A lovely way to get kids to eat offal without them knowing. The chicken livers impart a lovely, rich, meaty earthiness and you want something sweet to go with that, which is why the apricot and honey sprouts work so well.

Serves 4

20g unsalted butter
3 garlic cloves, crushed
150g shallots, chopped
10g sage, chopped
salt and pepper
1.5 litres strong fresh chicken stock
    (or make it up from cubes)
200g chicken livers
200g vegetable suet
400g self-raising flour, plus a little
    extra for shaping the dumplings
English mustard, to serve

Apricot and honey sprouts
rapeseed oil, for frying
300g Brussels sprouts, peeled with
    the core cut out (think of them as
    baby cabbages), shredded
100g shallots, chopped
1 tbsp runny honey
2.5cm piece of fresh ginger, grated
2 tsp Dijon mustard
50g dried apricots, cut into 5mm pieces

1 Heat the butter in a pan over a low–medium heat then add the garlic, shallots and sage with some salt and pepper and leave to sweat gently for 5 minutes. Remove from the heat and leave to cool.

2 Bring the stock to a gentle simmer in a large pan. Purée the chicken livers in a blender or food processor till smooth then add to the shallot mixture.

3 In a large bowl, mix the suet and flour with a wooden spoon until thoroughly combined. Add the liver mixture and mix till you have a firm dough. Lightly flour your hands then divide the mixture into golf ball-sized pieces and roll into balls. Drop the dumplings into the gently simmering stock, cover and cook for 12 minutes (you may need to do this in two batches so that you don't overcrowd the pan). Remove from the cooking liquid with a slotted spoon. Leave stock on the heat to keep it hot..

4 Meanwhile, cook the sprouts. Heat a wok or large frying pan and coat the base with rapeseed oil. Throw in the sprouts and shallots and stir-fry till they get a wee bit of colour on them. Add the honey and shoogle (shake) the pan, then add the ginger, mustard and apricots. Check the seasoning and cook for 5 minutes.

5 Serve the dumplings in bowls with the sprouts, a jug of the cooking stock and some mustard on the side.

Dumpling tips
Dumplings need a proportion of half suet to flour. Always simmer dumplings; do not boil them, otherwise the mixture will break up. For extra-light dumplings, avoid lifting the lid during cooking.

Chicken casserole with cheese-scone topping

When I was growing up, anything with scones on top was a treat, whether it was a savoury casserole or a pud – it did nae matter, you just had this tasty topping that soaked up the lovely juices of what lay beneath. This one is no exception.

Serves 6-8

8 skinless, boneless chicken thighs
salt and pepper
1 tbsp rapeseed oil
200g cooking chorizo, broken into nuggets
24 button onions
4 garlic cloves, crushed
2 celery sticks, thinly sliced
150g button mushrooms, stalks removed
150g fresh or frozen baby carrots
1 leek, trimmed and cut into 2cm slices
400g cherry tomatoes
4 bay leaves
bunch of fresh thyme, tied with string
500ml chicken or vegetable stock
1 tbsp cornflour dissolved in 2 tbsp cold
    water

Scone topping
110ml buttermilk
1 egg
20g sage, chopped
175g self-raising flour
½ tsp cayenne pepper
good pinch of sea salt
50g unsalted butter, diced
100g mature Cheddar, grated

1. Preheat the oven to 200°C/gas 6.

2. Trim the chicken thighs of any fatty bits and cut each one in half. Season well with salt and pepper.

3. Heat the oil in a large ovenproof casserole over a medium heat. Fry the chicken, in batches, until lightly browned all over then remove from the casserole.

4. Put the casserole back on the heat and fry the chorizo, then add the onions, garlic and celery. Cook for 4–5 minutes over a medium–high heat, stirring regularly, until lightly coloured. Add the mushrooms and cook for 1 minute more, stirring.

5. Return the chicken to the pot along with the carrots, leek, tomatoes, bay, thyme and stock. Season and bring to the boil then reduce to a simmer, cover with a lid and cook in the oven for 30 minutes.

6. Meanwhile, make the topping. In a bowl, mix the buttermilk with the egg and sage. In a separate bowl, sift together the flour and cayenne pepper. Stir in the salt until everything is well mixed, then use your fingers to rub the butter in until it's all crumbly. Gently mix in the cheese, then gradually add the buttermilk mixture to the dry ingredients, mixing first with a knife then with your hands to make a soft dough. If it seems a little dry, add another ½ tablespoon of buttermilk, or enough to make a soft, smooth dough that will leave the bowl clean.

7. Roll out the dough as evenly as possible, to around 2.5cm thick – no less than this otherwise the scones won't rise well. Using a 7cm fluted cutter, stamp out the scones. Gently re-roll the dough and stamp out additional scones to use it all up.

8. Remove the casserole from the oven, check the seasoning then adjust the thickness of the sauce with the cornflour and water. Now cover the top of the casserole with the scones. Pop back into the hot oven and cook till the scones are golden brown and cooked through – about 30 minutes.

Duck stovies

This wonderful, amazing concoction that came out of Scotland and whose name is derived from the French *à l'étuvée* (steamed or braised) should grace more tables in the land! Woe to those who think it is a cheap, threadbare dish to use up any scrappy thing bound with tatties – no! It's a glorious, hearty dish based on lamb or mutton and beef, but always the trimmings – lamb belly or beef skirt – and here I have made it a little bit more contemporary with duck. The duck is confited and the fat is then used for the potatoes, and it's served with a bit of brown sauce and fried duck eggs on top – yes! Save any leftover duck fat – it can be kept in the fridge for up to a month and used to add bags of flavour to roast tatties.

Serves 6

Duck confit

1 tbsp fennel seeds
1 tbsp five-spice powder
2–3 bay leaves, (fresh or dried), chopped
150g sea salt
500g thyme sprigs
50g rosemary sprigs
zest of 2 oranges
20 garlic cloves, with skins, bashed with a rolling pin to bruise them
8 small duck legs
1 litre duck fat

Stovies

2 onions, finely chopped
3 garlic cloves, crushed
3 bay leaves
40g thyme sprigs, tied in a bunch with string
1kg floury potatoes, peeled and diced
about 300ml strong chicken stock (if you can get duck stock, all the better)
salt and ground white pepper
2 tsp chopped flat parsley
1 tsp chopped tarragon
3 tsp chopped chives

To serve

6 large duck eggs
brown sauce (I like HP), Chilli Sauce (see page 250) or Tamarind and Date Sauce (see page 243)

1. Mix the fennel seeds, five-spice powder, bay leaves, salt, thyme, rosemary, orange zest and garlic then rub the mixture into the duck legs. Place in the fridge and leave to marinate overnight.

2. The next day, preheat the oven to 120°C/gas ½.

3. Wipe off the duck legs, place in a roasting tin and pour the duck fat over them. Cook in the oven for 6 hours or until the bone pulls away from the meat easily.

4. Remove the duck legs from the fat and leave to cool. Pass the fat through a sieve while still hot. Pick all the duck meat off the bones.

5. In a heavy-based pan that will take all the ingredients and has a lid, place 100g of the sieved duck fat and allow to melt over a low heat. Add the onions and garlic and fry gently till the onions are translucent. Add the bay leaves, thyme and potatoes and season with salt and white pepper. Cover with a tight-fitting lid (to keep in all that steam and flavour) and cook on a low–medium heat for 15 minutes, stirring.

6. Stir in enough stock to cover the potatoes and bring to the boil, then turn the heat down to a low simmer and cook with the lid off until the potatoes are cooked through and breaking down into the liquid. Take the pan off the heat, stir in the parsley, tarragon, chives, picked duck meat and season again. Keep the lid on the pot and it will stay hot for ages.

7. Fry the duck eggs in hot duck fat until cooked to your liking and season with salt and pepper. Serve the fried eggs on a pile of the stovies along with sauce of your choice.

Peanut butter chicken thighs with caramelised nuts and steamed rice

Peanut butter? It sounds weird, but think of satay. This has the same essential elements; it's salty, sweet, crunchy, comforting and delicious.

Serves 6

2 tbsp soy sauce
1 tbsp rum
1½ tsp cornflour
800g boneless, skinless, chicken thighs, cut into 2.5cm cubes
1 tbsp peanut oil
Steamed Rice (see page 234), to serve
Caramel Spiced Nuts (see page 16), to serve

Sauce

1 tbsp Chinese black vinegar, or good-quality balsamic vinegar
200g crunchy peanut butter
1 tsp soy sauce
2 tbsp sesame oil
1 tsp Szechuan peppercorns, toasted then ground
8–10 small dried red chillies
6 spring onions, white and green parts separated, thinly sliced
6 garlic cloves, crushed
5cm piece of fresh ginger, peeled and finely chopped or grated
100g unsalted dry-roasted peanuts

1. Mix the soy sauce, rum and cornflour in a bowl. Add the chicken and mix well to ensure all the chicken is coated in the marinade. Leave to stand at room temperature for 10 minutes.

2. For the sauce, in another bowl, combine the vinegar, peanut butter, soy sauce, sesame oil and Szechuan peppercorns and mix until smooth.

3. Heat a wok or large heavy-based pan over a high heat. Add the peanut oil and swirl to coat the base. Add the chillies and stir-fry for about 30 seconds, or until the chillies have just begun to blacken and the oil is slightly fragrant.

4. Add the chicken and stir-fry until no longer pink – about 2–3 minutes. Add the white parts of the spring onions, the garlic and ginger and stir-fry for about 30 seconds. Pour in the peanut butter mixture and stir to coat the other ingredients. Stir in the peanuts and cook for another 1–2 minutes.

5. Serve the chicken and sauce on plates with the steamed rice, sprinkling over the green spring onion and the spiced nuts at the end.

Pictured overleaf

Thai crispy duck with orange, papaya and peanut salad

Fruit + duck = marriage made in heaven. Aromatic spices go so well with the crispy skin of the duck and you've got that lovely bright orange of the papaya in the salad. Pretty as a picture and deliciously tasty too!

Serves 4

4 tbsp Thai red curry paste
grated zest and juice of 2 limes
1 tbsp palm, muscovado
  or brown sugar
2 tsp Thai fish sauce
10 basil leaves, chopped
4 small duck breasts
100ml coconut milk
sea salt

Salad

3 large navel oranges
1 garlic clove, crushed
2 tsp Thai fish sauce
2 tbsp rice vinegar
4 tbsp rapeseed oil
1 large papaya, peeled and cut into
  cubes
4 large leeks, white part only,
  shredded and kept in iced water
  (to keep it crispy)
4 tbsp salted peanuts
2 tbsp chopped coriander

1. Put the curry paste, lime zest and juice, sugar, fish sauce and basil leaves into a small bowl and mix well. Pour into a shallow dish that will allow the duck to sit in the marinade without it touching the skin.

2. Prick the fleshy underside of the duck breasts all over with a sharp pointy knife so that the marinade can get in, then place the breasts in the marinade skin-side up. Leave for 24 hours if possible, or at least 8 if not.

3. Preheat the oven to 200°C/gas 6.

4. Lift the duck out of the marinade and wipe off the marinade, then pat the breasts dry with kitchen paper. Slash the skin in a criss-cross pattern with a small sharp knife – this will help release the fat from the skin as it cooks. Season the skin with salt and rub it in.

5. Heat a non-stick pan frying pan over a medium–high heat. Once the pan is hot, add the duck breasts, skin-side down. Fry for 3–5 minutes making sure that the fat runs out of the skin and that the skin is browning and crisping but not burning.

6. Remove the duck breasts from the pan and place them skin-side up in a roasting tray. Pat the skin with kitchen paper to remove any excess fat. Place the roasting tray on the middle shelf in the oven for 7 minutes.

7. Meanwhile, make the salad. Prepare the oranges by cutting away the peel and white pith, then cut out the segments between the membranes. In a large bowl, whisk together the garlic, fish sauce and vinegar. Once combined, drizzle in the oil and whisk until the mixture is emulsified. Gently stir in the orange and papaya and leave to stand at room temperature for 15 minutes.

8. After removing the duck breasts from the oven allow them to rest for about 2–3 minutes. Meanwhile, place the marinade in a pan and bring to a simmer. Add the coconut milk and bring back to a simmer. Taste and adjust the seasoning then switch off the heat.

9. To serve, slice the duck breasts. Drain the leeks and toss with the peanuts and coriander. Place the leeks on plates, then spoon over the orange salad. Top with the duck and spoon over some sauce.

Venison and haggis burgers with smoked Cheddar, chickpea and sweetcorn relish

They say most things can be traced back to childhood; well this one goes back to the thing that got me as a kid: burger envy! So, no beef, no worries: I came up with this recipe, which is now one of my favourites. You've got venison mince, which can be a bit dry, but it also contains lovely juicy, fat, spiced haggis, which adds loads of extra flavour and moisture to the burgers. A great one for the barbecue.

Serves 6

650g finely minced venison or beef
1 large onion, grated and squeezed dry
   in a tea towel
2 garlic cloves, crushed
70g curly parsley, chopped
1 egg
1 tsp salt
1 tsp ground pepper
400g haggis (don't be tempted
   by the tinned stuff; I use Campbells
   prime meat fresh haggis)
100g smoked Cheddar-style cheese,
   grated

Chickpea and sweetcorn relish

½ x 250g tin chickpeas
½ x 200g tin sweetcorn
150g red onions (about 2 onions),
   finely diced
3 dashes Tabasco sauce
1 tsp chopped tarragon
salt and pepper

Cumin mayo

2 tsp cumin seeds
200ml mayonnaise
salt and pepper
1 lemon

1. Place the venison mince, onion, garlic, parsley, egg, salt and pepper in a large bowl and mix well.

2. Take a little of this mixture and cook in a hot frying pan so that you can taste the seasoning and adjust if necessary. Then divide the remaining mince mixture into six balls of equal size and pop into the fridge.

3. Grate the haggis, mix it with the cheese and divide into six equal amounts. Take a mince ball and flatten it out on a piece of cling film to twice the size of burger size you're aiming for. Place a portion of the grated haggis mixture in the centre and bring the sides of the burger together and seal it over the haggis. Wrap in the cling film. Repeat with the rest of the burgers and put them in the fridge for an hour to firm up.

4. To make the relish, drain the chickpeas and discard the liquid. Take out a quarter, mash with a fork and place the remaining whole chickpeas in a large bowl. Drain the sweetcorn, discard the liquid and add to the chickpeas. Add the rest of the ingredients, including the mashed chickpeas, to the bowl and stir together well, checking the seasoning. This relish will keep for 4 days in the fridge.

5. To make the cumin mayo, toast the cumin seeds in a pan over a low heat till they change colour. Leave to cool and then grind. Mix with the mayonnaise, then adjust the seasoning as needed with salt, pepper and a squeeze of lemon juice. Refrigerate until needed.

6. Prepare the barbecue or preheat the oven to 170°C/gas 3½. Heat a frying pan and fry the burgers on each side, for about 5 minutes, until nicely coloured, then pop in the oven or on the barbecue for 7 minutes or until cooked to your liking. Serve with the relish and cumin mayo.

Krispy with a capital 'K' chicken wings

My favourite finger food. Get your mates round, get a big bowl of these crispy fried wings on the table, a few beers and loads of dips. I guarantee the wings will be hoofed in minutes and you'll have a happy bunch of well-fed diners.

Serves 4

1 tsp chilli powder
1 tsp ground cumin
½ tsp ground coriander
1½ tsp sweet paprika
½ tsp garam masala
2 tbsp onion powder (if you can't get this use vegetable stock powder)
1 tbsp garlic powder
1.5kg chicken wings, skin on, tips taken off and jointed
150g plain flour
75g cornflour
500–700ml vegetable oil,

To serve
Spice Mix (see page 248)
4–6 celery sticks (at least 1 per person), cut into slim short lengths
Tamarind and Date Sauce (see page 243)
Blue Cheese Sauce (see page 252),

1. In a large shallow dish, mix together the chilli, cumin, coriander, paprika, garam masala and onion and garlic powders. Add the chicken wings and rub the spice mixture into the meat. Cover and refrigerate for at least 8 hours, overnight if possible.

2. Mix the flours in a plate and gently coat each wing in the mixture. Shake off any excess.

3. Put a deep-fat fryer on to 190°C or fill a deep pan a quarter–half full with oil and heat.

4. Carefully add about 8 pieces of the chicken and cook, stirring and flipping the chicken occasionally, until golden brown and crisp – about 10 minutes total. Drain on kitchen paper and cook the remaining batches. (Adjust the heat of the oil to maintain a temperature of 180–200°C.)

5. Transfer the wings to a serving plate, sprinkle with the spice mix and serve with the celery sticks and the sauces alongside, for dipping.

Pictured overleaf

03 FISH SUPPERS

I have always loved seafood – in all its wondrous shapes and sizes – and in Scotland I'm lucky to be able to enjoy an amazing selection of locally fished varieties.

As kids, my brothers and sisters and I would revel in the fact that we were eating exotic sea monsters. I grew up eating squid, octopus, crabs and mussels, species that all sound very tame and normal today but that in the 1970s in Edinburgh were wild and weird.

In spite of our situation, the only Scottish fish dish my mum made was her take on fish and chips; others were cooked with spices, chilli, garlic and tomatoes – ingredients that weren't common to fish preparation at the time but reflected our Indian heritage.

Fish doesn't need to be fussed about with. Whether baked, grilled, fried, barbecued or poached, all fish needs is to be seasoned well and cooked for the right length of time to retain its moisture. A squeeze of lemon and/or a knob of butter is often enough if it's jazzed up with the veg and accompaniments you're serving alongside. But to make it truly special, I'd encourage you to turn to my Pandora's Box chapter (see pages 229–52) to find a spice mix or a sauce or salsa that can really lift it to a whole other level.

The seafood recipes here are not complicated, nor have I chosen expensive varieties. In the main, I've gone for seafood that's local to me and have paired it with flavours you might not have thought of. I couldn't not include a fish pie, but it's not your everyday classic; and even my favourite – fish and chips – has been spiced up.

Roast sardines with Lebanese lentils

Sardines were called pilchards when I was growing up. I loved them, but some people used to turn their nose up at them because of their name, which apparently sounded unappetising. Now that they're called sardines, it's a different story, and I do think that with these Lebanese-spiced lentils and preserved lemons, they make a fantastic dish you won't refuse.

Serves 6

180g Puy lentils
50g unsalted butter
1 red onion, chopped
2 garlic cloves, crushed
12 large sardines, gutted and scaled

Dressing

1 preserved lemon, from a jar
4 tbsp olive oil
3 tbsp pomegranate molasses
  (you want one that is more sweet
  than sour)
4 spring onions, finely sliced
50g fresh ginger, peeled and chopped
juice and zest of 1 lemon
25g mint leaves, chopped
25g flat-leaf parsley leaves, chopped
salt and pepper

1   Preheat the oven to its highest temperature.

2   Place the lentils in a pan of cold water. Bring to the boil and simmer for around 25–30 minutes, or until they are just done. Drain and leave to cool.

3   Melt the butter in an ovenproof frying pan, then fry the onion and garlic together for 5 minutes. Pop the sardines on top of the onion and garlic and put in the oven for 8 minutes, or until the sardines are coloured and cooked.

4   To make the dressing, cut the preserved lemon into quarters, discard the flesh, wash the rind and finely chop. Place in a bowl with the olive oil, pomegranate molasses, spring onions, ginger, lemon juice and zest, mint, parsley and seasoning and whisk together.

5   Put the lentils in bowl. They are ready to serve as a side or main event, hot or cold, but to make them special for this dish, remove the sardines from the pan and scrape all the onions and juices from the cooking into the lentils. Add the dressing and mix well. Place the sardines on top of the lentils to serve.

Fish 'n' chips
with tamarind mushy peas

In Scotland, a 'fish supper' is fish and chips – 'supper' is slang for basically any meal from the chippie served with chips. There are different accompaniments depending on where you find yourself, but if you're in Edinburgh, like me, your fish supper has got to be served with 'sauce' or 'chippy sauce', an amazing ambrosial mix of Gold Star brown sauce mixed with a splash of vinegar (or sometimes water). Sooo tasty! I've given you a recipe for my take on trying to recreate the sauce and it's almost as good as the real deal. By my reckoning, the Deep Sea chippie at the top of Leith Walk sold the best fish and chips in the world – it was Eddie's succulent battered haddock that got me hooked on all things fishy. I've moved the concept up a gear here using my friend Cyrus's recipe – he marinates the fish in a top-notch spicy marinade before battering it. Cheers Cyrus! There are some great brands of oven chips around at the moment, so just pop a batch in the oven while you make the fish and knock up the obligatory mushy peas.

Serves 4

4 x 150g haddock fillets
vegetable oil, for deep-frying
plain flour, for dusting

Marinade
juice of 2 limes
1 tsp ground turmeric
1 tbsp ground coriander
1 tsp chilli powder
4 cloves garlic, crushed
1 tbsp Worcestershire sauce
2 tsp salt

Batter
400g self-raising flour
1 tsp baking powder
500ml cold water
salt and pepper
50ml vinegar

1 Mix all the marinade ingredients together in a bowl. Rub all over the fish fillets and place on a plate or tray that fits in the fridge. Pour all the marinade over the fish and leave in the fridge for as long as possible before you use it.

2 For the batter, mix the flour and baking powder together in a bowl, make a well and whisk in the cold water till you have a thick batter. Season well then whisk in the vinegar.

To serve
chunky oven chips (they need to be
  fat!)
Chippy Sauce (see page 241)
1 double quantity of Mushy Pea and
  Tamarind Purée (see page 129)

3 To cook the fish, put a deep-fat fryer on to 180°C or heat enough oil in
a deep saucepan. Wipe any excess marinade from the fish. Dust the
fish with plain flour, shake off any excess and dip the fish in the batter, then
shake off any excess batter. Place the fish carefully into the hot fat. Cook for
6–7 minutes, or until golden brown. Remove with a slotted spoon and drain
on kitchen paper, then repeat with the remaining fillets.

4 Season the fish with fine salt and serve with the chips, chippy sauce
and the mushy pea and tamarind purée.

Pictured on pages 88–89

Going Goan gone fish pie

I just can't help mixing up cuisines and cultures and playing about with tried-and-trusted recipes. So, with apologies for the bad pun, this is simply a Goan-inspired twist on one of Britain's favourites. I've spiced the pie mix up with coconut milk, chilli and tamarind, but at its heart it's still good old comfort food. For the photo, we played about serving it in enamel mugs and individual pie dishes, but you can just as easily bake it in a single dish – I've given the instructions below. You could also decorate the pie with cooked prawns still in their shells.

Serves 4

1 tbsp coriander seeds
1 tsp cumin seeds
3 tbsp vegetable oil
2 onions, finely chopped
1 dried red chilli
½ tsp ground turmeric
1½ tbsp peeled and finely chopped
    fresh ginger
5 garlic cloves, peeled and crushed
1 x 200g tin chopped plum tomatoes
1 fresh green chilli, chopped
1 tsp salt
1 x 400ml tin coconut milk
600g pollock, skinned and cut into
    chunks
300g cooked peeled prawns
2 tsp tamarind extract
fresh coriander leaves, to garnish

Mash topping

500g floury potatoes (King Edward,
    Maris Piper, Wilja, Ailsa or Golden
    Wonder), roughly chopped
salt
100g butter
15g coriander, chopped
150g mature Cheddar, cut into
    1cm cubes

1 Start by making the topping. Place the potatoes in a pan, cover with water, add salt and bring to the boil. Boil the potatoes for about 14–16 minutes or until very soft, then drain well. Return to the pan and leave them to steam and dry out in the heat of the pan. Mash well, either with a ricer or just with a fork until the mash is as smooth as you can get it. Transfer to a clean pan and place over a low heat to cook out any additional moisture. Stir in the butter and season well. Remove from the heat and stir in the coriander and cheese. Leave to one side until you are ready to top the pie(s).

2 Preheat the oven to 200°C/gas 6.

3 Toast the coriander and cumin seeds in a dry pan until aromatic. Grind to a powder in a spice grinder or pestle and mortar.

4 Heat 2 tablespoons of the oil in a large pan over a medium–high heat, then add the onion and fry till golden brown. Add the toasted spices, chilli and turmeric and cook for a minutes, stirring all the time. Add the ginger and garlic and fry for another 2 minutes, then stir in the tomato, green chilli and salt and cook until most of the liquid has evaporated.

5 Add the coconut milk and bring to the boil, then simmer for about 10 minutes to infuse the flavours. Taste for seasoning. Add the fish, prawns and tamarind extract, bring back to the boil then simmer for 3 minutes, or until the fish is only just cooked. Divide between four 400ml individual pie dishes or a 1.75-litre pie dish. Top with the coriander mash and bake in the oven for 10 minutes, or until golden brown.

Also pictured overleaf

Ras el hanout-rubbed pollock with caramelised chicory

Ras el hanout is a spice mix from North Africa and means 'head of the shop' in Arabic, which implies a mixture of the best spices the seller has to offer. I think of it as the garam masala of Morocco as it can be made up of anything from 10 to 100 different spices. This is a very good one made by a great friend of mine, Saleem, who worked with me at the Balmoral Hotel in Edinburgh – it's his mother's recipe and I think it's the best I have ever tried. If you're stuck, a ready-made shop mix is a good alternative.

Serves 4

Fish
4 x 175g pollock fillets, skinned
1½ tbsp Ras el Hanout (see page 245)
zest and juice of 1 large orange
3 tbsp cold-pressed vegetable oil
salt
2 tbsp finely chopped flat-leaf parsley
1 tsp chopped fresh thyme
lemon wedges, to serve

Caramelised chicory
45g unsalted butter
2 heads chicory, halved lengthways
  and core removed
2 tsp clear honey
juice of 1 large orange
salt and pepper

1 Preheat the oven to 200°C/gas 6.

2 For the caramelised chicory, use an ovenproof dish that will take the chicory snugly but without overlapping. Rub half the butter thickly over the bottom and then pack the chicory into the dish. Drizzle over the honey and orange juice and season with salt and pepper. Dot with the remaining butter.

3 Roast the chicory in the oven, uncovered, for about 1 hour, turning and basting every 10 minutes. Keep a close eye on proceedings towards the end of the cooking time and take the dish out of the oven when the juices have reduced to a few spoonfuls of thick syrup and the chicory is looking suitably caramelised.

4 Meanwhile, place the fish on a baking tray, and gently rub the surface with the ras el hanout, making sure to coat the fish evenly all over.

5 Whisk the orange zest, juice and vegetable oil together in a bowl with a pinch of salt. Pour over the fish then bake in the oven for 10–15 minutes, depending on the thickness.

6 Serve the fish on top of the chicory and pour over the marinade. Garnish with the chopped parsley and thyme and serve with lemon wedges.

Slow-cooked hake, peppers and coriander

This slow-cooked hake and pepper dish was introduced to me by Humberto, one of the barmen at my Oloroso restaurant, who was from Lisbon. He was a fantastic mixologist but also a dab hand at cooking. This is one of his mum's recipes, adapted a little here. Pomegranate molasses comes in different strengths – some brands are sweeter than others; some are quite sour so you may need to add a little sugar to the sauce to balance the flavour.

Serves 4

5 tbsp olive oil
½ red pepper, finely sliced
½ yellow pepper, finely sliced
½ green pepper, finely sliced
½ orange pepper, finely sliced
½ fennel, finely sliced
2 red onions, chopped
4 garlic cloves, crushed
1 red chilli, finely chopped
1 bouquet garni (6–8 thyme sprigs
    tied up with 3 bay leaves)
salt and pepper
2 tbsp pomegranate molasses
200g tin chickpeas, drained
1 tsp sugar, or to taste
4 x 200g darnes of hake (cut through
    the bone, scaled and trimmed),
    with skin
40g coriander, chopped

1. Preheat the oven to 180ºC/gas 4.

2. Heat the olive oil in a casserole or ovenproof dish with a lid that will take all the ingredients. Add the peppers, fennel, onion, garlic, chilli, bouquet garni and a pinch of salt. Bring to a sizzle on top of the stove, pop on the lid and cook for 3 minutes.

3. Transfer the dish to the oven, cook for 10 minutes, then turn down the heat to 120ºC/gas ½ and cook for 45 minutes until soft, stirring from time to time. Add the molasses and chickpeas and stir in well. Check the seasoning and add the sugar if necessary. Place the hake on top of the stew, put the lid on and pop back in the oven for 35 minutes.

4. When the fish is cooked, lift the fish off the stew and set aside. Bring the pan juices and pepper to a quick boil on the stove top, stir in the coriander and serve with the fish back on top of the stew.

Or swap in ...
Instead of the darnes, you can buy fillets of hake without the bone or any other firm-fleshed fish in season.

Gurnard
with spicy sausage and lentils

Gurnard is the ugly, unloved fish of the UK and as such it can be cheaper than
other fish. So this is budget nosh at its best: hearty, cheap ingredients like lentils
and simple veg, pepped up with some herbs. Simple yet super tasty.

Serves 4

3 tbsp vegetable oil
1 large onion, thinly sliced
4 garlic cloves, crushed
1 carrot, thinly sliced
1 celery stick, thinly sliced
2 bay leaves
20g thyme
200g Merguez sausage, chopped
   into chunks
200g brown lentils, washed in cold
   water until it runs clear
1 x 400g tin chopped tomatoes
about 350ml fish stock (fresh or made
   with a cube)
100ml red wine
sea and pepper
4 skinless gurnard fillets
2 tsp chopped tarragon
2 tsp chopped chives
2 tsp chopped dill
20g flat-leaf parsley, chopped

1 Heat 2 tablespoons of the oil in large heavy-based pan or casserole
over a medium heat. Add the onion and garlic and cook slowly until soft
and translucent, then add the carrot, celery, bay leaves, thyme and sausages
and cook for 5 minutes, until the sausages are nicely browned.

2 Add the lentils, tomatoes, 350ml of stock, wine, salt and pepper to the
pan. Bring to the boil, cover and simmer very slowly for about 1 hour, or
until the lentils are soft. Check the pan every so often to make sure that it is
not getting too dry. Add a little more stock if necessary.

3 Towards the end of the cooking time, heat the remaining tablespoon
of oil in a frying pan and fry the gurnard fillets (in batches, if necessary)
till the pieces are golden brown all over. Remove and set aside.

4 When the lentils are cooked, stir in the herbs and season to taste.
Place the gurnard pieces on top and continue to cook with the lid on
for 4–5 minutes, until the gurnard is warmed through.

Hot smoked salmon kedgeree with vodka crème fraîche

Kedgeree is an Anglo-Indian dish that is thought to have come back from the Raj. A portly general trying to recreate what they were used to in India, perhaps – a bit of spice and rice. Let's make it truly British and have some smoked fish with it. This dish is wonderful on a cold morning, just before your hunting, fishing or shooting trip… That's if you're a general, of course.

Serves 6

60g unsalted butter
1 onion, finely chopped
3 garlic cloves, crushed
2 tsp chopped fresh ginger
½ tsp ground turmeric
¼ tsp chilli powder
2 tsp garam marsala
basmati rice, measured up to the
   450ml mark on a measuring jug
finely grated zest of 1 large lemon
570ml fish stock
500g skinless hot-smoked salmon,
   such as Salar hot-smoked salmon
   from the Hebrides or if this is to
   difficult to find or expensive use
   peat-smoked haddock
3 large eggs, hard-boiled, cooled and
   roughly chopped
4 spring onions, roughly chopped
2 tbsp mixed chopped herbs (such
   as chives, parsley, dill, chervil,
   lemon balm)
sea salt and freshly ground black
   pepper
lemon wedges, to serve

Vodka crème fraîche
200g crème fraîche
35ml vodka
Tabasco sauce, to taste

1. Melt the butter in a medium heavy-bottomed saucepan. Choose one that has a well-fitting lid. Soften the onion in the butter, allowing it to cook for a few minutes. Add the garlic, ginger and spices and keep stirring for 3 minutes.

2. Add the rice, lemon zest and a good pinch of salt. Stir well, until the rice is coated, then pour in the fish stock. Bring to the boil and immediately cover with the close-fitting lid, or a layer of foil plus the lid, then turn the heat down to very low. Leave for exactly 15 minutes then turn the heat off, but do not remove the lid from the rice for at least a further 10 minutes. Don't cheat and be tempted to look before 10 minutes are up!

3. While the rice is cooking, flake the fish into a large mixing bowl. Check that no bones have made it into the mixture. Add the hard-boiled egg and spring onion.

4. For the vodka crème fraîche, pour the crème fraîche, vodka, a good pinch of salt and 8 drops of Tabasco sauce into a chilled bowl (add more Tabasco if you like it hotter). Whisk – either by hand or with an electric whisk – to soft peaks. Transfer to a serving bowl.

5. Once the rice is cooked, add it to the salmon mixture. Fold the ingredients together well – it is easiest to do this with a large metal spoon. Stir in the chopped fresh herbs and check the seasoning (remember the smoked fish will add saltiness to the finished dish), adding freshly ground black pepper. Serve with wedges of lemon and the crème fraîche on the side for your guests to help themselves. Eggy joy.

Baked salmon parcels

It might sound a bit weird using maple syrup in a fish dish, but the sweetness of the syrup with its little metallic notes on the tongue is great when combined with the other flavours – chilli, fresh ginger, pickled ginger, coriander – perfect for cutting through the richness of the salmon. Serve each person their own parcel to open at the table – I like to write my guests' names on the parcels or draw pictures on them.

Serves 4

4 tbsp maple syrup
juice of 1 lime
1 tbsp chopped fresh ginger
1 tbsp chopped coriander
1 tbsp chopped dill
½ red Thai chilli, chopped
4 x 170g salmon fillet, skinned and boned
1 tbsp sesame oil
8 spring onions, sliced finely
1 red pepper, deseeded and finely sliced
4 tsp chopped pickled ginger
sea salt and freshly ground black pepper

1 Preheat the oven to 200°C/gas 6.

2 In a bowl mix the maple syrup, lime juice, fresh ginger, herbs and chilli and put to one side.

3 Rub the salmon with the sesame oil then season each fillet.

4 Take four sheets of greaseproof paper and divide the spring onions and red pepper between them, putting them in the centre of the foil. Place each salmon fillet on top and divide the pickled ginger between them. Bring the sides of the paper up and crimp the sides to create an open parcel, pour on the maple mixture, then seal the tops of the parcels.

5 Place on a baking tray in the oven to cook for 10–15 minutes, or until the salmon is cooked. Serve the salmon directly from the parcel, so the guests get that great aroma when they open up the fish.

Fish burger with soda bread and cucumber pickle

Fish-cake mix is the trimmings your fishmonger is left with after portioning up the fish he sells. It's such good value as you're buying a mixture of great-quality fish at a knock-down price – perfect for tossing together with other flavours to make a juicy, tasty fish burger.

Serves 4

400g fish-cake mix from your fishmonger, skinned and boned (if you can't get that go for 200g salmon plus 200g white sustainable fish)
1 tbsp Thai red curry paste
2 garlic cloves, crushed
juice of 1 lime
2 mackerel fillets, skinned, boned and finely chopped
½ medium red onion, finely chopped
3 spring onions, finely chopped
2 gherkins, finely chopped
2 tbsp chopped coriander leaves
1 tbsp finely chopped dill
plain flour, for dusting
olive oil, for frying
salt and pepper
soda bread (home-made, see page 235, or shop-bought), to serve
butter or mayonnaise, to serve
Pickled Cucumber and Tomatoes (see page 236), to serve

1 Place the fish mix (not the mackerel) in a food processor, with the curry paste, garlic and lime juice and pulse to a coarse paste. Transfer to a bowl.

2 Mix in the mackerel, red and spring onions, gherkin, coriander and dill and season well. Test fry a little bit of the mixture to check the seasoning if you think you need to. With floured hands, shape the mixture into 4–6 burgers. Chill in the fridge for 1 hour to firm up.

3 Heat 1 tablespoon of olive oil in a frying pan over a medium heat and fry the fish burgers, two at a time, adding more oil to the pan if you need to. Cook for about 5 minutes on each side, or until nicely browned and crispy.

4 To serve, slice the soda bread (in half if using farls) and spread it with lashings of butter or mayonnaise. Layer the pickle on to the bottom half of your sandwich, top with a burger then another slice/the lid of your soda bread.

Fish skewers with Balinese spices and pineapple sambal

A sambal is a condiment that is served as you would a chutney and its ingredients are cooked for just a few minutes to retain their freshness and vibrancy. There are literally thousands of different kinds served across South East Asia and they are a great way of pepping up a dish. This pineapple sambal is dead simple to make and makes these meaty fish skewers sing. It's a great fallback to serve with any grilled fish and can be kept in the fridge for up to a week. Serve the skewers with some boiled rice and/or a crisp watercress salad.

Serves 4

7 small shallots, peeled and quartered
6 garlic cloves, peeled
5cm piece of fresh ginger, peeled and chopped
3 red chillies, deseeded
1 tsp turmeric
1 tbsp Thai fish sauce
2 lemongrass stalks, trimmed of just the bottom bulb and the top stalk
pinch of ground cloves
½ nutmeg, grated
1 tbsp brown sugar
2 tsp coriander seeds
½ tsp black peppercorns
2 tbsp vegetable oil
800g white fish, such as pollock, cut into equal-sized cubes about 4–5cm

1. Put the shallots, garlic, ginger, chillies, turmeric, fish sauce, lemongrass, cloves, nutmeg and sugar in a food processor and pulse till you have a rough purée. Leave in the machine.

2. Toast the coriander seeds and black peppercorns in a dry frying pan till fragrant, then crush to a coarse powder using a pestle and mortar. Add to the garlic mixture and pulse again.

3. Heat the oil in a heavy-bottomed pan and, when hot, add the paste and fry till golden and fragrant. Take off the heat and leave to cool.

4. Pour the paste over the cubes of fish and mix well. Skewer on to metal or soaked wooden skewers, pop into a shallow dish and place in the fridge for as long as you can.

Pineapple sambal

3 large shallots, peeled, halved
    lengthways and thinly sliced
    crossways
2 garlic cloves, finely chopped
2 long mild red chillies (5–8cm long),
    finely chopped
2 tbsp Thai fish sauce
3 tbsp vegetable oil
4 dried red chillies
100ml coconut milk
1 medium pineapple (you want a really
    sweet one), peeled, cored, and cut
    into 1cm cubes
juice of 2 limes
3 tbsp chopped coriander
sugar, to taste
salt

5 For the sambal, pureé the shallots and garlic in a food processor and put to one side. Do the same with the fresh chillies and fish sauce and put to one side.

6 Heat the oil in a wok or heavy-based pan. Add the dried chillies and stir-fry for 1 minute then remove the chillies from the oil. Add the shallot purée and fry for 3 minutes, then add the chilli and fish sauce mix and keep cooking until fragrant – about 5–10 minutes. Add the coconut milk, bring to the boil and simmer until the oil splits from the sauce. Take off the heat, add the pineapple, lime juice and coriander and allow to cool. Check the seasoning, adding salt and sugar to taste.

7 Heat your overhead grill on the highest setting. Grill the fish skewers for about 8–10 minutes, turning twice and brushing with more marinade as you go. Check the fish is opaque in the centre then serve with the pineapple sambal.

Pictured overleaf

Salt cod tattie scone with caper mayo and watercress salad

As you may have guessed, I am a tattie scone devotee. Well this is a posher version, made with salt cod. The scones are a great starter or snack on their own, but to make them into a yummy lunch or brunch dish add a soft poached egg. The mayo isn't difficult to make, and I think it's really worth making your own, but if you want to cut out this step, just stir the capers and lemon zest through shop-bought mayo.

Serves 6

250g salt cod
milk, enough to cover the cod by 2.5cm
3 bay leaves
6 peppercorns
1 bunch of thyme
1 garlic bulb, cut in half horizontally
500g floury potatoes, (such as King
 Edward or Maris Piper), unpeeled
50g butter, plus an extra knob for
 frying the scones
175g plain flour, plus extra to dust
salt and pepper
vegetable oil, for frying
6 poached eggs, to serve (optional)

Caper mayo
2 medium egg yolks
½ tsp salt
1 tbsp vinegar (I like to use sherry
 vinegar but you can use one of your
 own favourites)
1 tsp English mustard
about 250ml sunflower oil (it depends
 on how thick you want your mayo)
salt and pepper
sugar, to taste
zest of 1 lemon, plus juice, to taste
150g capers in vinegar, rinsed in cold
 water and squeezed, roughly
 chopped

1 You will need to soak your salt cod in plenty of water for 24–48 hours, changing the water four times during the process.

2 To make the caper mayo, place the egg yolks, salt, vinegar and mustard in a blender and pulse briefly to combine. With the motor running, add the oil in a slow, steady stream. The mayonnaise will start to thicken; when it is thick enough for your liking, stop the machine. Adjust the seasoning with salt, pepper, sugar and a squeeze of lemon juice, if necessary. Stir the capers and lemon zest into the mayo then check the seasoning again.

3 Drain and rinse the salt cod, then pop it into a pan with enough milk to cover it by 2.5cm. Add the bay leaves, peppercorns, thyme and garlic. Slowly bring to the boil over a low–medium heat, then remove and leave the fish to cool in the milk. Once cool, drain and flake the fish.

4 Put the potatoes in a pan, cover with water, salt generously and bring to the boil. Simmer until cooked through, then drain well. Peel off the skins as soon as you can handle them and return the potatoes to the pan on a low heat to dry them off. Stir with a wooden spoon for about 8 minutes, until really dry.

5 Transfer the potatoes to a bowl, add the butter and flaked salt cod, then stir in the flour and season to taste. Roll out the dough on a lightly floured surface to about 5mm thick, then cut around a 15cm side plate to shape – you should get about 6 scones.

To save time ...
Instead of making your own mayo, you can simply stir the lemon juice and capers into 200g of shop-bought mayo.

Watercress salad

2 tbsp extra-virgin olive oil

squeeze of lemon juice

salt and pepper

pinch of caster sugar

2 large bunches of watercress, stalks
  trimmed

2 shallots, peeled and thinly sliced

6 Prepare the salad dressing by whisking the olive oil and lemon juice then seasoning to taste with salt, pepper and sugar. In a bowl, mix the watercress and shallots, drizzle over the dressing and toss.

7 To cook the scones, pour a dash of vegetable oil into a large heavy-based frying pan and place over a medium-high heat. Add a small knob of butter and when the butter is foaming, fry one scone disc at a time until golden on both sides – about 3–5 minutes in total. Repeat with the remaining scones, adding more oil or butter to the pan as you cook each one. Cut into triangles and serve immediately, with a poached egg on top if you wish, and the salad and caper mayo.

Pictured overleaf

Thai fish cake Scotch egg

It's been said that Scotch eggs came from India; at least, this is what my friend Mr Cyrus Todiwala tells me. *Nargisi kofta* is an egg covered in fine lamb mince. Here I have taken the concept a step further away from its origins. This recipe is for a wee quail's egg, wrapped in fish pâté and spiced with Thai spices: India meets Blighty meets Thailand.

Serves 8

24 quails' eggs, at room temperature
500g skinless fish-cake mix from
    fishmonger
1 tbsp finely chopped coriander
½ tbsp chopped mint
½ tbsp finely chopped parsley
½ tsp finely chopped tarragon
1 tbsp Thai green curry paste
2 medium eggs, 1 left whole, 1 beaten
4 tbsp plain flour
100g dried breadcrumbs
vegetable oil, for frying
salt and pepper

Dipping sauce
4 tbsp sweet chilli sauce
4 tsp lime juice
1 chopped bird's eye chilli
1 tbsp chopped mint

1 Carefully lower the eggs into boiling water. Cook for 2½ minutes, then rinse under cold water and leave in cold water for 10 minutes to cool completely. Peel.

2 Mix the fish with the chopped herbs, curry paste and whole egg and season well. Place in a food processor and whizz to get a semi-smooth mixture. Divide the mixture into 24 balls, then flatten each into a circle.

3 Make sure the eggs are dry then dust with flour. Use your hands to mould the fish mix around each egg, ensuring there are no gaps.

4 Roll each egg in flour, then in beaten egg wash, then in breadcrumbs. Chill until ready to cook.

5 Make the dipping sauce by mixing all the ingredients well.

6 Heat about 8–10cm of vegetable oil in a frying pan until hot. Carefully fry the eggs in batches of three, turning them as you fry so that they cook evenly, until they are crispy and have some colour. Serve warm with the dipping sauce.

Also pictured overleaf

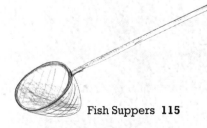

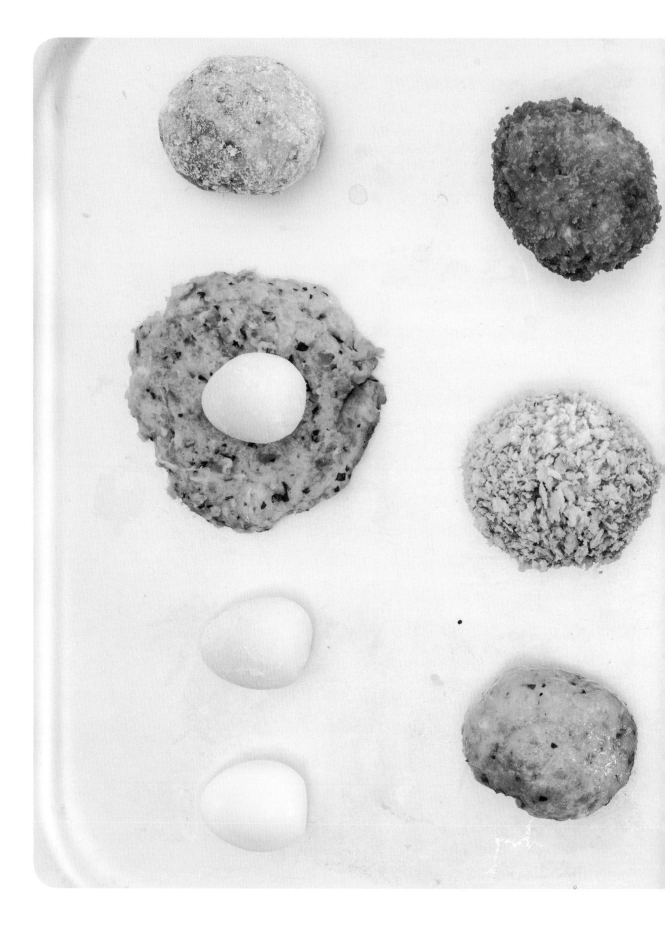

Pickled herring and herbed potato salad summer roll

Summer rolls – the raw Vietnamese equivalent of the deep-fried Chinese spring roll, stuffed with salad and prawns – can be a bit of a chic foodie kind of thing, a bit posh. But here I've brought them right back to the bedsit kitchen by using pickled herrings. It really works! The contrast of flavours and textures; the sharpness of the pickled fish combined with soft potato, crunchy veg and peanuts and fresh herbs inside the squidgy rice wrapper is … well, you just have to try it.

Serves 4

8 rice paper (spring roll) wrappers
120g rocket
150g new potatoes, boiled in their
    skins, then cooled and sliced into
    thin discs
4 shallots, sliced lengthways as thinly
    as possible
16 mint sprigs, leaves only
16 coriander sprigs, leaves only
16 sprigs of Thai basil, leaves only
1 carrot, peeled and cut into fine
    matchsticks
¼ cucumber, cut into fine matchsticks
150g drained pickled herrings,
    unrolled, stuffing discarded
¼ iceberg lettuce, shredded, plus a few
    extra leaves
4 tbsp salted roasted peanuts, roughly
    chopped

For the Thai dipping sauce:
1 tbsp caster sugar
2 tbsp lime juice
1 tbsp Thai fish sauce
1 garlic clove, crushed
1 bird's eye chilli, finely chopped

1 Set out all the prepared ingredients within easy reach of your work area in plates or bowls.

2 Half fill a bowl big enough to fit the wrappers inside it with cold water. Drop in a wrapper and keep patting it for about 30 seconds, until it's pliable, but not completely soft. Lay it flat on your work surface or a chopping board and pat dry with kitchen paper.

3 About 2.5cm in from the bottom edge of the wrapper, start to layer the roll filling. Lay down a horizontal line of rocket, then cover it with potato slices. Top with shallot rings, then the herb leaves. Add a few carrot and cucumber sticks then the herring. Finish with some shredded lettuce and a line of chopped peanuts.

4 Bring the bottom edge of the wrapper tightly up over the filling, and then fold the sides in over it. Roll up tightly and place on a plate, join-side down. Repeat, covering the finished rolls with lettuce leaves to keep them fresh.

5 Once all the rolls are made, make the sauce. Whisk the sugar into the lime juice to dissolve, then add the remaining ingredients. Adjust to taste if necessary.

Chilli bream with harissa

All I can say, and will keep saying, is fish tastes so much better on the bone – all flavour from the bones goes into the fish and they keep the flesh wonderfully moist. This is a great recipe for preparing ahead. You can get most of the work done before your guests arrive and just pop it in the oven when you're ready to go. If you can't get hold of bream, it works wonderfully with sea bass or gurnard – anything you can buy on the bone.

Serves 4

4 sea bream, cleaned and scaled
8 thyme sprigs
6 garlic cloves, finely sliced
4 cinnamon sticks, crumbled
splash of white wine
good extra-virgin olive oil, to serve
salt and pepper

Harissa

1 tbsp ground coriander seeds
1 tbsp ground caraway seeds
1 tbsp ground cumin seeds
1 heaped tsp ground nutmeg
½ tsp ground cinnamon
2 level tsp sweet smoked paprika
250g long red chillies, split, deseeded
   and roughly chopped
3 rose petals (you want a fragrant rose;
   optional but tasty)
8 garlic cloves
1 sweet red pepper, roasted, peeled
   and seeded
1 tbsp tomato purée
1 tbsp sherry vinegar, plus extra to
   taste
6 tbsp extra virgin olive oil

1. For the harissa, mix all the spices together and toast in a dry pan over a medium heat till fragrant. Pop the chillies in a food processor and pulse. Add the remaining ingredients and blend to paste that is as smooth as possible. Check the seasoning and adjust with salt, pepper and more vinegar. Harissa keeps well in the fridge for a couple of weeks, but be sure to cover it with a little olive oil to seal it from the air.

2. Preheat the oven to 200°C/gas 6.

3. Make three slashes on each side of the fish, season inside and out and rub the harissa over all the fish inside and out.

4. Lay out four large pieces of foil, big enough to form a parcel round the fish, and lightly oil the centre.

5. Divide the thyme, garlic and cinnamon between the foil pieces – this is the bed for the fish. Put the sea bream on top, drizzle some olive oil inside and over the top of the fish. Fold up the foil and pour a splash of wine into each parcel. Scrunch together the edges of the foil to make a teepee, leaving enough space for the fish to steam – it must not be 'wrapped' in the foil.

6. Place the parcels on a baking tray and cook in the oven for 20 minutes. Serve the parcels on warmed plates and take to the table – it's lovely to open them there and have all the wonderful smells escape.

Smoked mackerel and chickpea burgers with ratatouille relish and mushroom ketchup

This dish is lovely but the real star of the show is (shhh, don't tell anybody) the ratatouille relish, which can be eaten hot, warm or cold. Once you've got this one down, you will be eating it with everything. Just make sure you chop everything first as the cooking of the relish is fast and furious! It does take time to chop everything into wee cubes but it is worth it. The mushroom ketchup is a fresh relish that should be kept in the fridge and used within a week or two.

Serves 4

Mushroom ketchup
350g Portabello mushrooms (if unavailable, use button mushrooms)
3 garlic cloves, peeled
3 tbsp cider vinegar
3 tbsp caster sugar
1 red onion, finely chopped
15 anchovy fillets
3 large gherkins
½ fresh red chilli, chopped
1 tsp Szechuan peppercorns
1 tsp ground paprika
2 tsp Dijon mustard

Ratatouille relish
5 tbsp olive oil
2 red onions
1 aubergine
1 red pepper
1 yellow pepper
½ fennel bulb
1 large courgette
4 garlic cloves, crushed
2 heaped tbsp tomato purée
salt and pepper
½ tsp sugar
4 tbsp sherry vinegar
½ tsp chopped rosemary
bunch of basil, chopped

1 To make the mushroom ketchup, put everything in a food processor and whizz until you have a fine mixture. Scrape into a heavy saucepan, place over a moderate heat and bring to the boil, stirring. Turn down to a simmer and cook for 25–30 minutes to thicken. Check the seasoning – you want a sharp, sweet, salty mix.

2 For the ratatouille relish, finely chop the red onions and cut the aubergine, peppers, fennel and courgette into 5mm dice. Put your widest pan on a high heat – ideally you want a pan with a base that will take all of the mix in one go. If not, use your biggest pan and cook in batches. Heat the pan for 5 minutes and then add the oil – it should be smoking right away. Add all the vegetables and garlic and stir-fry for 1 minute. Add the tomato purée and keep cooking on the highest heat for another 3 minutes, stirring every 30 seconds. Take off the heat, season with salt, pepper and the sugar and add the vinegar, rosemary and basil. Check the seasoning again.

Burgers

125g dried chickpeas, soaked in plenty
   of water overnight
1 red onion, very finely chopped
1 tbsp capers, squeezed dry
1 tbsp gherkins
3 garlic cloves, crushed
1½ tsp ground cumin
1 tbsp roughly chopped parsley
1 tbsp roughly chopped dill
1 tbsp roughly chopped basil
¼ tsp chilli powder
2 tbsp gram flour
1 tsp salt
350g smoked mackerel, flaked, with as
   much of the skin removed as possible
oil for deep frying

 For the burgers, drain the chickpeas thoroughly and pulse in a food
processor until lightly broken up. Add all the remaining ingredients
except the fish and oil and continue to pulse until you have the texture of
coarse breadcrumbs. Mix in the fish by hand. With oiled hands, gently form
the mixture into 4–6 burgers, each weighing about 150g.

Heat the oil until very hot, then shallow-fry the burgers until crisp and
golden. Serve with the ratatouille relish and mushroom ketchup.

Tuna on the hoof

A sandwich in a recipe book? Well, this isn't just any old tuna sandwich – it's got all the essentials: mayo, crisp lettuce, and spring onions, but the special touches are the Shichimi Togarashi and the tuna – fresh steaks, sliced thinly and made to kiss a hot grill. At a push you can use tinned tuna, just please don't use the sad stuff in sunflower oil or brine: use tuna in olive oil, such as Ortiz, which has an incredible flavour. And at the very least, make sure you use skipjack tuna that has been pole and line caught.

Serves 4

500g pole- and line-caught tuna steak
splash of vegetable oil
8 thin slices sourdough bread, crusts on
unsalted butter, softened (no marge, no spreads – trust in cows, not chemists!)
mayonnaise
½ iceberg lettuce, torn
salt and pepper
½ cucumber, peeled and thinly sliced
splash of olive oil
sprinkling of Shichimi Togarashi (see page 135)
1 spring onion, finely sliced

1. Slice the tuna into 16 slices (or ask your fishmonger to do this for you). Rub one side of the slices with vegetable oil and put them to one side.

2. Thinly butter half the bread slices then spread the remaining slices with a thin layer of mayonnaise.

3. Lay the lettuce on half the bread slices and sprinkle over a bit of salt, then place the cucumber on top followed by some black pepper.

4. Heat a non-stick pan or grill plate. Sear the tuna slices, oil-side down, for less than 40 seconds, then remove from the pan and pop on a plate. Sprinkle the tuna with olive oil and a light dusting of shichimi togarashi. Place on top of the cucumber, scatter over some spring onions and top with the other slices of bread. And there you have it: your tuna sandwich of joy.

Baked fish fingers with a surprise

If only my school dinners had included these ... I would have been such a good boy.

Makes 14–16 fat fish fingers

250g panko breadcrumbs
1kg skinless haddock fillet, cut into
   fingers about 12 x 4cm
3 tbsp rapeseed oil
salt and pepper
2 medium eggs
Caper Mayo (see page 110) or
   Aioli (see page 248), to serve

Mushy pea and tamarind purée
50g unsalted butter
2 tsp tamarind extract
1 tbsp caster sugar
salt and pepper
1 x 300g tin mushy peas

1. Preheat the oven to 220°C/gas 7.

2. Start by making the mushy pea and tamarind purée. Melt the butter in a pan, add the tamarind, sugar, some salt and lots of black pepper. Keep on the heat for 2 minutes then remove and mix in the mushy peas. Place in a bowl to cool.

3. Lay the breadcrumbs out in a thin layer on two baking trays and toast them for 6-8 minutes until lightly golden. Remove and leave to cool.

4. Spoon a line of the cold pea purée down the middle of a haddock finger and sandwich another finger on top. Repeat till all the fish is used up. If you have any purée left over you can serve this on the side. Pop the fish sandwiches in the fridge.

5. Tip the breadcrumbs into a large bowl, break them up, then toss with the oil and plenty of salt and pepper until evenly and lightly coated. Beat the eggs in a shallow bowl.

6. One at a time, dip the fish fingers into the beaten egg and then into the breadcrumbs to coat. Arrange them in one or two large oven trays, spaced slightly apart. Place in the oven and bake for 10 minutes, or until crisp and lightly golden. Serve with caper mayo or aioli.

Potted shrimp in spiced butter with sourdough

This is a British classic; I'm just turning up the volume a little. The star of the show is still the brown shrimp, but with the extra heat and a wee kick from the ginger, you can carry this off on hearty toasted sourdough rather than the traditional Melba toast (really, really thin pieces of crisp toast) – or you could even make your own sourdough Melba toast.

Serves 4

300g unsalted butter
1 bay leaf
6 black peppercorns
juice of 1 lime
¼ tsp ground mace
¼ tsp white pepper
½ tsp anchovy paste
1 finger chilli, split lengthways and
   seeds removed
1 bunch thyme
pinch of salt
2.5cm piece fresh ginger, just bruised
200g cooked and peeled brown shrimp
   (if you can't get these, use cold-water
   prawns or cooked crab meat)
sourdough toast, to serve

1 Place the butter in a heavy-based pan with the bay leaf and peppercorns and melt slowly over a low heat. Keep cooking until foamy on the top, then remove the pan from the heat and let stand for 5 minutes.

2 Skim the foam from the top and slowly pour the remaining liquid, bay and peppercorns through some muslin, or two sheets of kitchen paper, into a container.

3 Pour two thirds of this clarified butter into a clean pan over a medium heat. Add the lime juice, mace, white pepper, anchovy paste, chilli, thyme, ginger and a pinch of salt and simmer very gently for 5 minutes, then take off the heat and allow to cool but not set.

4 Divide the shrimp between four ramekins, packing them firmly in. When just warm, but still liquid, divide the spiced butter between the ramekins and put in the fridge to set.

5 Once solid, pour over the remaining clarified butter (if it has set, warm it up but make sure it's not hot or it will melt and sink to the bottom of the ramekin) and return to the fridge to set. Serve with lots of hot sourdough toast.

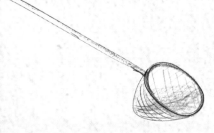

Tiger prawns with grilled chorizo, rocket and parsley

Cuisines collide yet again. The chorizo and hot paprika are inspired by Spanish cooking while jalapeños are a variety of Mexican chilli. They can range from mild to moderately hot and here they give the accompanying mayo just a little kick – lovely alongside the sweet prawns and spicy chorizo.

Serves 6

1kg raw tiger prawns, heads
   and shells on
100ml vegetable oil
5 garlic cloves, crushed
3 banana shallots, finely chopped
200g fresh chorizo sausage, chopped
   into 2.5cm cubes
1 tsp plain flour
1 tsp hot paprika
150ml sherry
salt and pepper
2 tbsp chopped flat-leaf parsley

Salad
rocket leaves (enough for 4 people)
2 banana shallots, finely chopped
1 red pepper, finely chopped

Chipotle mayo
juice of 1 lemon
150g drained jalapeño peppers
   (from a jar)
1 tsp ground cumin
200g mayonnaise
salt and pepper

1   To make the chipotle mayo, combine the lemon juice, jalapeño peppers, cumin and mayonnaise in a blender. Pulse to a purée and season to taste with salt and pepper.

2   Give the prawns a rinse in cold water for a couple of minutes, then pop them into a colander to drain.

3   Take a large frying pan that is wide enough to hold all the prawns in a single layer. Heat the oil over a medium heat and add the garlic, shallots and chorizo. Cook until the oils come out of the chorizo and the onion is translucent but not browned.

4   Add the flour and paprika and stir-fry for 20 seconds. Add the sherry, cook for 3 minutes and then add the prawns to the pan. Turn up the heat and shake the pan vigorously, tossing the prawns a couple of times. Season to taste and stir in the parsley. Cover and cook for 3–4 minutes, until the prawns have turned pink and are cooked through.

5   To serve, place the rocket and chopped shallots and pepper in a bowl. Toss with the juices from the prawn pan, then dish out and put the prawns on top. Serve the mayo alongside for everybody to help themselves.

Chilli and ginger squid with crispy garlic and broccoli and beansprout salad

Get a tempura batter right and you will be tempura-ing anything you can – it's so easy to do, so more-ish and, once you've got your head round handling hot oil, quick and super tasty. This is the batter I've devised, but it's the same mix you'll find in a pre-mixed packet so do just buy one of those if you'd prefer. My other bit of advice for getting tempura right is buy a decent slotted spoon so that you can lift your treasure out the oil easily.

Serves 4

500g squid (ask your fishmonger
    to clean it for you), sliced into 3cm
    pieces
200g plain flour, seasoned with
    1 tsp salt and ¼ tsp chilli powder
lime wedges, to serve
Spice Mix (see page 248),
    to serve

Tempura batter
120g rice flour
80g cornflour
10g baking powder
200ml iced water

Crispy fried garlic
4 large garlic cloves, peeled
vegetable oil, for deep frying
salt

Salad
juice of 2 limes (measure it)
40g stem ginger, chopped
toasted sesame oil, same quantity as
    lime juice
150g beansprouts
150g sprouting broccoli, blanched
    and thinly sliced

1 Start with the crispy garlic. Slice the garlic as thinly as possible using a small slicer or a mandolin. Heat 5cm vegetable oil in a heavy-based pan to 170ºC. To test the temperature of the oil, add a slice of garlic. If it sizzles, add the rest of the garlic in three batches and cook until just crisp and light golden brown – a matter of seconds. Use a slotted spoon to keep the slices moving as they cook so they don't stick. Once golden brown and crispy, transfer the garlic to kitchen paper to drain, then sprinkle with salt.

2 For the tempura batter, combine the rice flour, cornflour and baking powder in a bowl and then stir in the water to make a thick batter – it should have the consistency of double cream.

3 Put a deep-fat fryer on to 165ºC or fill a deep pan a quarter-full with oil and heat.

4 Pat dry the squid and form into four piles. Dredge one pile through the seasoned flour and shake off any excess. Then dredge through the tempura batter. Deep-fry for about 4 minutes, until golden brown, then take out and put on a tray lined with kitchen paper to drain. Repeat with the other three piles of squid.

5 For the salad, mix the lime juice with the stem ginger and sesame oil in a large bowl. Toss the broccoli and beansprouts together in this dressing. Pile the squid on top and sprinkle with the crispy garlic. Serve with lime wedges and the spice mix on the side.

Crayfish and Gruyère macaroni

What is better than cheese and macaroni? Answer: crayfish in your macaroni cheese – it turns it into a rich, decadent dish. I've used three types of cheese in my version: Cheddar for tang; Gruyère for melty stringiness and mascarpone for creaminess. You could swap the two hard cheeses for your own favourites if you prefer.

Serves 6

200g butter
200g plain flour
250ml semi-skinned milk
250ml single cream
4 shallots, finely chopped
50g mild Cheddar, grated
150g Gruyère cheese, grated
50g mascarpone
250g crayfish in brine, drained
350g dry macaroni, boiled until al dente,
   and cooled

Crunchy crust
2 tbsp butter
2 garlic cloves, crushed
150g panko breadcrumbs
1 tbsp chopped parsley
1 tbsp chopped chives
1 tbsp chopped tarragon
zest of 1 lemon
1 tbsp vegetable oil
2 tbsp grated Parmesan
salt and pepper

1. Preheat the oven to 200°C/gas 6.

2. To make the crunchy crust, melt the butter in a heavy-based pan. Add the garlic and sauté for 1–2 minutes. Add the panko breadcrumbs, all the herbs, the lemon zest and vegetable oil, and fry for 1 minute. Take off the heat and put in a bowl. Add the Parmesan and season with salt and pepper.

3. Melt the butter in a large saucepan over a medium heat. Add all the flour, stir into the butter to blend and cook for 2–4 minutes, stirring. Mix the milk and cream together in a jug and slowly add to the butter and flour mixture until it thickens. When this happens, turn down the heat, add the shallots and cook for 8 minutes. Add the three cheeses to the sauce and mix well. Take off the heat, add the crayfish and season.

4. Mix the sauce with the pasta, put in an ovenproof dish, top with the crunchy crust and pop in the oven for 8–10 minutes, until golden brown and crispy on top.

Crab and sweet potato cakes with Japanese mayo

People think of Japanese food as really clean and delicate, but it has a saucy side as well. This Japanese mayo uses shichimi togarashi, a chilli-based, seven-spice dusting that I use quite a lot. Once you've got it ready-made in a jar you will find yourself sprinkling it on top of all sorts of things. The recipe is below but you can get pre-made mixes from Asian supermarkets and they are spot on.

Serves 6

200g mayonnaise
1 tbsp lemon juice
350g sweet potatoes, peeled and cut
  into chunks
2 tbsp olive oil
salt and pepper
3 garlic cloves, peeled
1 red pepper, cut into 2cm dice
350g crabmeat (mix of white and brown
  meat – I use dressed crabs and
  scoop out the meat)
20g parsley, chopped
2 spring onions, chopped
200g plain flour, plus extra for dusting
100g semolina
2 tbsp dry breadcrumbs, if needed
vegetable oil, for frying

Shichimi togarashi

2 tsp white sesame seeds, toasted
3 tsp Szechuan peppercorns
2 sheets nori (seaweed)
3 tsp dried tangerine or orange peel
3 tsp chilli powder
1 tsp black sesame seeds, toasted
1 tsp poppy seeds, toasted

1. Preheat the oven to 180°C/gas 4.

2. To make the shichimi togarashi, grind the white sesame seeds and Szechuan peppercorns coarsely in a spice grinder or using a pestle and mortar. Add the nori and dried peel and grind again briefly. Stir in the remaining ingredients and blend well. Place the spice mix in a jar as you will have plenty left over to use in other recipes.

3. Put the mayonnaise in a bowl and stir in the lemon juice and 2 teaspoons of the shichimi. Taste and add more shichimi if needed. Cover and refrigerate until needed.

4. Place the sweet potatoes in a roasting tin and toss with olive oil, salt and pepper. Roast in the oven for about 20 minutes.

5. Take the roasting tin out of the oven, add the garlic and red pepper and cook for another 10 minutes.

6. Mash the cooked vegetables with a fork or potato masher to obtain a rough mixture. Once cool, add the crab meat, parsley and onions, mixing well.

7. Mix the flour and semolina, then dust your hands with flour and shape the mixture into six individual cakes. If the mix is too wet add a tablespoon or two of dry breadcrumbs. Lightly dust the cakes all over with flour.

8. Heat enough oil for shallow-frying in a pan, then fry the cakes over a medium–high heat in two batches, until golden brown on both sides. Serve with the Japanese mayo.

04 VEGGIE

The world has changed a lot for vegetarians. When I was growing up in the 1970s, being vegetarian was hard. Finding unusual and exciting fresh vegetables wasn't always easy, and unless you were lucky enough to come from a background where there was a culinary history of being inventive with exotic spices, pulses and vegetables to make really tasty dishes, vegetarian food was bland and tasteless.

And when I started cooking, vegetarians were not really catered for in restaurants either. Worse, if you had someone come into a restaurant and say they were vegetarian, a groan would emerge from the kitchen and the poor veggie would probably get nut cutlets as a main with a salad or soup to start. The pudding, whether it did or didn't contain gelatine, would be deemed fit, 'cos there's no real meat in it, son', my senior chef would say to me. After seeing this, I wanted to make sure I would always provide food with sparkle for vegetarians.

The experience also taught me two things: one, respect your customer, and two, show the same respect for vegetables and pulses as you would give to the more 'glamorous' ingredients like meat and fish.

So, with this in mind, I hope the dishes in this chapter need no further introduction; their veggie glory should satisfy and sustain and make sure no vegetarian – or carnivore – is ever left wanting.

Goats' cheese and beetroot tacos

A great veggie supper that came about after I made mini tacos for a canapé party on the Royal Yacht Britannia at which the Mexican consulate was being entertained. Although roasting your own beetroot really brings out its flavour, you could use pre-cooked shop-bought beetroot (just not the stuff in vinegar please!) to make this even easier to throw together.

Makes 8 tacos

4 raw beetroot
1 small onion, peeled
1 Granny Smith apple, peeled
1 garlic clove, crushed
salt and pepper
2 tbsp sultanas
2 tbsp vegetable oil
1 tsp cumin seeds
1 tbsp sherry vinegar
250g goats' cheese log, crumbled
8 taco shells
Avocado Cream (see page 45)
2 tbsp pine nuts
mustard cress, to garnish (optional)

1　Preheat the oven to 160°C/gas 3. Prick the beetroot all over, place on a baking tray and bake for about 40–45 minutes, until cooked through but still slightly firm – a sharp knife should slide in easily. Leave to cool.

2　Once the beetroot is completely cool, peel then grate it into a large bowl, then grate in the onion and apple and mix well. Add the garlic, salt and pepper to taste and the sultanas and mix again.

3　Preheat the grill to high. In a small pan, heat the oil till smoking, then take off the heat and add the cumin seeds. They will fizz up and change colour very quickly but don't worry. As soon as this has died down, pour the seeds over the beetroot, add the sherry vinegar and mix well.

4　Place the goats' cheese on a baking tray lined with baking paper and grill until browned.

5　Divide the beetroot between the taco shells, then cover with the avocado cream, then the pine nuts, goats' cheese and finally the mustard cress (if using).

Aubergine flatbreads with mint and coriander chutney

The step of chargrilling the aubergine is so important to add that lovely, smoky flavour. This is then imparted through the hot flatbreads when they come off the griddle, ready to be dipped in your mint yoghurt – tasty.

Serves 4–6 (makes 12)

Aubergine filling

2 aubergines
2½ tsp olive oil
2 small red onions, grated and
    squeezed to remove extra moisture
4 garlic cloves, crushed to a purée
    (or use 1 tsp garlic purée)
1 tsp tomato purée
10g coriander chopped
1 tbsp sherry vinegar
½ tsp caster sugar
salt and pepper

1 Start by making the filling. Hold the aubergines over an open flame on your hob, or pop them under the grill on its highest setting, and cook until charred and burnt all over (this will impart a wonderful smoky flavour to the filling). Put the aubergines in a bowl of cold water until you can handle them, then peel of all the burnt and charred skin – it should just fall away. Cut off the tops and roughly chop up the aubergine flesh.

2 Heat the oil and fry the grated onion for 5 minutes without letting it colour, then add the garlic and tomato purée and cook for another 5 minutes. Add the aubergine and cook for 10–15 minutes on a medium heat, making sure that you stir constantly so that it doesn't stick. Take the mixture off the heat and stir in the coriander, vinegar and sugar. Set aside to cool completely while you make the flatbread dough.

3 Warm the water until lukewarm then mix in the yeast and oil.

4 In a large, warm mixing bowl, add the flour and salt to the water, then mix with your hands to bring the mixture together. Mix to a soft dough.

5 Put the dough on a lightly floured board and knead for 5–10 minutes. When the dough feels smooth and silky, place it back in the mixing bowl, cover with a warm tea towel and leave in a warm place to rise until the dough has doubled in size.

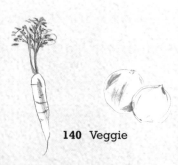

Flatbread dough

about 300ml water
10g fast-action yeast
1 tbsp rapeseed oil, plus extra for
  cooking the flatbreads
500g strong white bread flour
10g salt

To serve

Mint and Coriander Chutney (see page
  239)

6　Tip the dough on to a floured surface. Knock back the dough then divide into 12 equal pieces and roll into balls. Set aside.

7　Make an indentation in the centre of each ball of dough and put a couple of heaped teaspoons of the aubergine mixture into the hollow then pinch the dough over like a money bag to seal. Repeat with the remaining pieces of dough.

8　Place a ball of the stuffed dough on a well-floured work surface and flatten with a rolling pin into a disc or oval about 16cm in diameter. Place on a baking sheet and repeat with the remainder. Put the baking sheet of flatbreads in a warm place for 10–15 minutes.

9　Brush a heavy-based frying pan or griddle with oil and place over a medium heat. Place two or three flatbreads into the pan, depending on the size of the pan, and cook for 3–4 minutes until coloured underneath (like a naan) then flip over and do the same again. Serve right away with the mint and coriander chutney.

Pictured overleaf

Hot tofu Caesar salad

This came about when I had a vegetarian mate round and was about to chuck some anchovies into the salad I was preparing… He looked a bit shocked and I suddenly realised what I was doing, quickly changed tack and swapped them for this tasty marinated fried tofu. Traditionalists will no doubt be horrified that I've messed with this iconic dish, but despite what they (or tofu sceptics) might think, this marinated fried tofu has got bags of body and loads of flavour, and it adds a totally different dimension to the classic salad.

Serves 4

4 tbsp hoisin sauce
2 tbsp sesame oil
350g firm tofu, cut into bite-sized cubes
2 heart of Romaine lettuces, roughly
  chopped
vegetable oil, for frying
8 tbsp croutons
Parmesan shavings, to garnish

Caesar-ish dressing
200g thick mayonnaise
4 tbsp grated Parmesan
2 garlic cloves, peeled
2 tbsp sherry vinegar
6 tbsp boiling water
1 tsp sugar
salt and pepper

1 In a bowl, mix the hoisin sauce and sesame oil. Add the tofu, mix well and leave to marinate for 15 minutes.

2 To make the dressing put all the ingredients in a food processor, or use a stick blender, and whizz till the garlic has been mashed up. Taste and season with salt and pepper if needed.

3 In a large bowl, toss the lettuce with as much dressing as you like (any left over will keep in the fridge for a week). Mix well and pop in a serving bowl.

4 Place a non-stick pan over a medium heat. Add a touch of vegetable oil to the pan then brown the tofu on all sides. Toss over the salad then garnish with the croutons and Parmesan.

Mac 'n' cheese

You have to give it to the Americans when it comes to jazzing things up: Cheese and Macaroni sounds nice, but mac 'n' cheese sounds so much better – and this is a killer one from a Scot.

Serves 4–6

350g dry macaroni
4 tomatoes, cut in half through the middle and core removed
1 tsp sugar
2 tbsp Worcestershire sauce
salt and pepper
600ml milk
150ml single cream
6 bay leaves
few sprigs fresh thyme
70g butter
6 garlic cloves, crushed
1 heaped tsp English mustard
70g plain flour
180g Cheddar, freshly grated
100g Parmesan, freshly grated
½ tbsp chopped parsley

1 Preheat the oven to 180°C/gas 4.

2 Cook the macaroni as directed on the packet, drain, put back in the pan and put to one side.

3 Place the tomatoes, sugar and Worcestershire sauce in a bowl, add salt and pepper to taste and mix well. Leave to one side.

4 Place the milk, cream, bay leaves and thyme in a pan, bring to the boil, then turn off the heat.

5 Melt the butter in a separate heavy-based saucepan. Add the garlic and mustard and cook for 2–3 minutes, then stir in the flour and cook for 2–3 minutes, stirring all the time so the mix does not stick or burn. Keep stirring the roux and gradually whisk in the milk mixture until you have a smooth sauce. Simmer for 5 minutes, whisking constantly until thickened (it doesn't matter about lumps or the herbs as you will pass the sauce through a sieve before using). Stir in all the Cheddar and half the Parmesan, check the seasoning, then pass through a sieve onto the pasta and stir well.

6 Pour the macaroni cheese into an ovenproof dish and arrange the tomatoes on top. Pour any juices from the tomato bowl over the pasta as well, sprinkle with the rest of the Parmesan, then pop in the oven and bake until golden brown – about 10 minutes. Take out of the oven, sprinkle with parsley and serve.

Sweetcorn and ginger dumplings

This is an easy dish and the filling can be changed for whatever else takes your fancy. Fun, fast and tasty! The shiitake broth is a great quick soup that can be used as the base for many dishes. Any leftover dumpling filling can be frozen to use another time or you can buy a second packet of wrappers, make extra dumplings and freeze them – they can be cooked from frozen in a simmering stock or broth.

Serves 4–6

Dumplings

150g firm tofu, diced
1 x 200g tin sweetcorn, drained
4 spring onions, sliced
3 garlic cloves, crushed
1 Serrano chilli, stalk trimmed,
    split in half
30g coriander (leaves and stems),
    chopped
1 tsp finely chopped ginger
2 tbsp sesame oil
salt and pepper
1 pack wonton wrappers
1 egg, beaten

Shiitake broth

1.2 litres water
4 garlic cloves, crushed
7.5cm piece fresh ginger, washed
    and smashed
1 finger chilli, split, seeds discarded
    and finely chopped
30g vegetable stock powder (I use
    Marigold bouillon powder)
250g shiitake mushrooms, sliced
4 spring onions, finely sliced
2 tbsp chopped coriander

1   To make the dumplings, mix all the ingredients except the wonton wrappers and beaten egg together in a large bowl. Taste and adjust the seasoning.

2   Lay out six wonton wrappers and keep the others in a pile covered with a damp cloth. Spoon one teaspoonful of filling in the middle of each wrapper then use a pastry brush to moisten all around the edge of the wrapper with the beaten egg. Bring the sides of the wrapper up over the filling and press together to seal. Repeat until the mixture is used up, setting the finished dumplings on a plate dusted with cornflour or plain flour. Keep in the fridge until needed.

3   To make the shiitake broth, pour the water into a pan, add the garlic, ginger and chilli and bring to the boil. Simmer for 5 minutes, then add the stock powder and simmer for a further 5 minutes. Pass the stock through a sieve into a clean pot, bring to a simmer, add the mushrooms and cook for 3 minutes. Add the dumplings and simmer for 10 minutes. Add the spring onions and coriander just before you serve the broth.

Sweet potato skirlie rolls with Desperate Dan beans

Skirlie derives from mealie pudding, which was a steamed savoury pudding made with oatmeal, onion and suet. Skirlie uses the same ingredients but they're cooked in a pan with bacon or meat fat. It was originally served with boiled fish and meats but is now more traditionally used as a stuffing for roasted poultry. I think it has so much more potential. Here it's mixed with sweet potatoes and used to fill puffed pastry. I serve it with jazzed-up, spiced baked beans.

Serves 4–6

2 sweet potatoes
150g butter
2 Spanish onions, finely chopped
30g thyme, leaves only
4 garlic cloves, crushed
500–600ml boiling vegetable stock
   (I use Marigold cubes)
200g pinhead oatmeal, lightly toasted
   in a dry heavy-based frying pan
20g flat-leaf parsley, chopped
500g puff pastry
1 egg, beaten
poppy seeds, to finish
2–3 batches of Desperate Dan beans
   (see page 26), to serve
brown sauce (I like HP), to serve

1   Preheat the oven to 200°C/gas 6.

2   Prick the sweet potatoes all over, place on a baking tray and bake for about 40–45 minutes, until cooked through but still slightly firm. Leave to cool then cut into 2cm cubes, leaving the skin on. Increase the oven setting to 220°C/gas 7.

3   Melt the butter in a large saucepan and cook the onion and thyme until soft and golden. Add the garlic and cook for 3 minutes, then add the oatmeal and mix well. Cook for about 5 minutes, stirring frequently.

4   Add the boiling stock a ladleful at a time and stir over a medium heat until the stock has been absorbed by the oatmeal and it is soaked but firm. Immediately remove from the heat and transfer to a large bowl. Add the diced baked sweet potato and the chopped parsley, season and mix well.

5   Line a large baking sheet with baking paper. Place the pastry on to a lightly floured work surface, split it into three equal portions and roll each out to a rectangle about the size of an A4 sheet of paper (30 x 20cm) and about 3mm thick.

6   Place a line of the skirlie mixture down the middle of each pastry rectangle, then brush each with beaten egg on one edge.

7   Fold one side of the pastry over onto the egg-washed side. Press down to seal with a fork and trim any excess. Repeat with the other rectangles.

8   Place the rolls on to a baking tray, brush with beaten egg and sprinkle poppy seeds over the tops. Bake for 30–35 minutes or until the pastry is golden-brown.

9   About 15 minutes before the end of the cooking time, prepare the beans (or reheat if you've already made them). Serve the skirlie rolls with the beans and brown sauce.

Halloumi skewers with peach and chilli relish and hazelnut dukkah

My kids call halloumi squeaky cheese. I admit I've never been a huge fan – I find it a little bit too salty – but this recipe convinced me. The firm texture of the cheese and, yes, its saltiness really work with the sweet peaches in the relish and the crunchy, spicy hazelnut dukkah.

Serves 4

1 tbsp olive oil
juice of 1 lemon
1 garlic clove, crushed
2 tsp chopped mint
750g halloumi cheese, cut into large chunks
2 small courgettes, halved lengthways and cut into large chunks
1 large red onion, cut into wedges, leaves separated
16 cherry tomatoes, halved
Hazelnut Dukkah (see page 249), to serve
Peach and Chilli Relish (see page 237), to serve

1 Mix the oil, lemon juice, garlic and mint in a bowl. Pop the cheese and all the veggies in the bowl and mix well so that everything is covered.

2 Heat an overhead grill, griddle pan or barbecue.

3 Thread the cheese and vegetables on to four to six skewers then grill for 6–7 minutes, turning them a few times to brown all over. Sprinkle the skewers with a good amount of dukkah and serve with the peach relish.

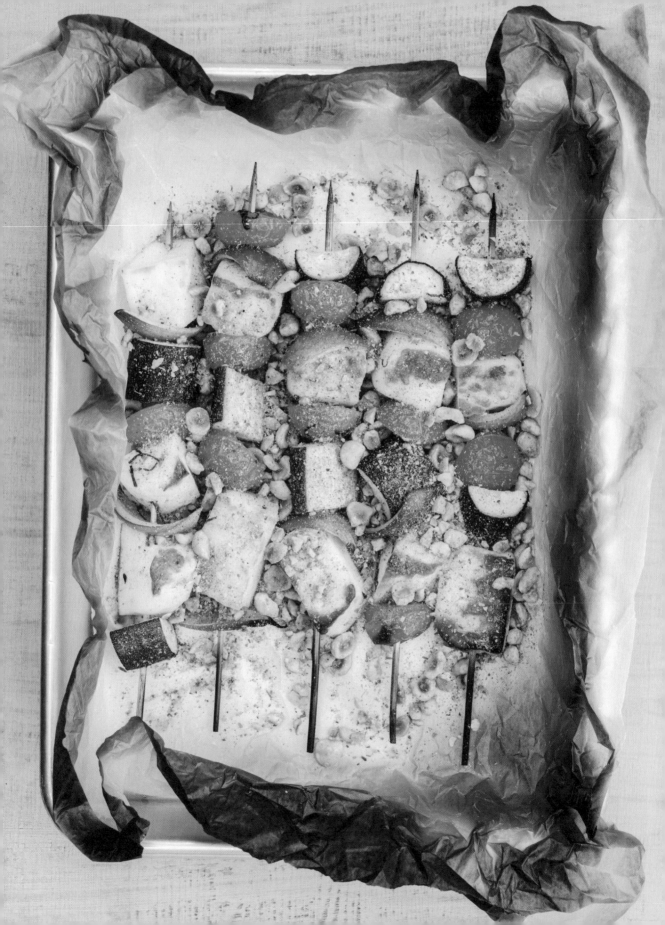

Rumbledethump croquettes with celeriac slaw and charred sweetcorn relish

'Rumbledethump' is a fantastic Scottish word and a dish from the Borders: 'rumble' means to toss and mix and 'thump' is to mash and bash. So, mash up tatties and parsnip, toss them with some greens, then shape them into little breaded croquettes and fry them. Woe betide anyone who calls this a Scottish version of bubble and squeak – to my mind this is so much more…

Makes 12 croquettes, to serve 4

400g Maris Piper potatoes, cut into small chunks
100g parsnips, cut into chunks half the size of the potato chunks
1 tbsp rapeseed oil
50g unsalted butter
1 onion, finely chopped
3 garlic cloves, crushed
150g Brussels sprouts, base removed and shredded (or use chopped spring cabbage)
½ tsp salt
½ tsp pepper
¼ tsp cayenne pepper
grated nutmeg, to taste
3 eggs
1 tbsp chopped curly parsley
2 tsp chopped tarragon
½ tsp thyme leaves
100g plain flour, plus extra for dusting
150ml milk
150g dried breadcrumbs

1   For the celeriac slaw, whisk together the vinegar, lemon juice, egg yolk, mustard, salt and lots of ground pepper in a large bowl, then slowly whisk in the oil. Add the celeriac, apple, shallots and tarragon. Mix well and check the seasoning.

2   For the sweetcorn relish, char the corn over an open flame of a hob or barbecue or under the grill – you want a good char on them to offset the sweetness. Slice off all the corn and put in a bowl. Add the other relish ingredients and season. Refrigerate the relish and slaw until needed.

3   Place the potatoes and parsnips in a pan, cover with cold water and bring to the boil. Cook until tender, then drain well. Mash – it's okay for it to have some lumps in it – then pop it into a bowl and leave to cool.

4   Heat half the oil and all the butter in a frying pan, add the onion and garlic and fry until tender but not coloured. Stir in the Brussels sprouts and cook for 3–4 minutes until wilted. Add this mixture to the mashed potatoes and parsnips and season with salt and pepper, caynee and nutmeg. Beat 1 egg in a bowl with the fresh herbs and add into the potato mixture. Mix well.

5   Dust your hands with flour and shape the mixture into 2.5 x 10cm croquettes. Keep dusting your hands with flour so the mix does not stick to your hand.

Celeriac slaw

2 tsp white wine vinegar
juice of 1 lemon
1 egg yolk
1 tbsp Dijon mustard
salt and pepper
150ml rapeseed oil
400g peeled celeriac, cut into
  matchsticks
2 golden delicious apples, peeled,
  cored and cut into matchsticks
3 shallots, finely chopped
1 tsp chopped tarragon

Charred sweetcorn relish

2 corn cobs
1 small red onion, finely chopped
1 red pepper, finely chopped
100ml Satan's Ketchup (see page 170)
juice and zest of 1 lime
salt and pepper

6 Place in the freezer for about 2 hours to firm up – this also makes it much easier to cover them in breadcrumbs.

7 To bread the croquettes, beat the remaining eggs and mix with the milk. Place this egg wash in a shallow bowl, then place the flour and breadcrumbs into separate bowls. Season the flour with salt and pepper. Dip each croquette first into the flour (shaking off the excess), then into the beaten eggs and milk, then into the breadcrumbs. Dip into the egg and then the breadcrumbs again and place on a tray until they are all done.

8 Put a deep-fat fryer on to 180°C or fill a deep pan a quarter full with oil and heat. Fry the croquettes in batches of four to six, depending on how big your fryer or pan is, for 5 – 7 minutes, or until golden brown. Serve with the celeriac slaw and charred sweetcorn relish.

To save time ....

To speed up the slaw, you can skip the stage of making your own mayo and simply stir the celeriac, apple, shallots and tarragon into 200g of shop-bought mayo.

Bread soup

Bread soup might sound a bit weird and strange but it's a classic peasant dish cooked in many countries, usually at Lent. The Italians make *pappa al pomodoro* with stale bread, olive oil and tomatoes and *soupe crasse* with stale breadsticks and taleggio cheese, while the Germans tuck into *Fränkische Brotsuppe* – stale bread cooked in a sausage broth. These dishes might have evolved originally to use up a glut of fresh tomatoes or the broth left over from making bratwurst, but in today's cost-conscious kitchens, where eating healthily within a limited budget might not be that simple, the frugal principles still hold fast. That's why I've come up with my take on these wonderful soups, which are great for the pocket and the palate. Don't stop at these – keep experimenting.

Serves 4–6

2 tbsp olive oil
2 large onions, finely chopped
4 garlic cloves (or 1 good tsp of purée)
½ tsp chilli powder
2–2.5 litres water
500g stale bread (keep collecting it
   and popping it in the freezer
   or drying it and keeping it in an
   airtight tub)
6 tsp stock powder
vinegar, whichever type you have,
   to taste
salt and pepper

1   Heat the oil in a heavy-based pan over a medium heat and fry the onions till golden brown. Add the garlic and cook for a few more minutes. Add the chilli, pour in 2 litres of water and bring to the boil. Add the bread, bring to a simmer and cook until the bread has broken down. Add the stock powder and season with salt and pepper.

2   Blend until smooth then pop back in the pan. Check the consistency of the soup – you may need to add more water to thin it down – then add vinegar and sugar, to taste. This is the basic soup mix but you can follow any of the instructions opposite to make one of my variations.

Herby

Blend the basic soup with 100g mixed soft herbs, such as flat-leaf parsley, chives, tarragon and basil.

Tomatoey

When you have sautéed the onions, add 4 tablespoons of tomato purée for a rich tomato taste.

Truffly

Add 150g of sautéed button mushrooms and a splash of truffle oil for a bit of decadence.

Spicy

Once the soup is made fry 2 tsp cumin seeds, 2 tsp garam masala and ½ teaspoon of chilli powder in 1 tbsp of oil until fragrant. Stir through for a spicy heart-warming soup

Aromatic

Once the soup is made heat 2 tbsp of toasted sesame oil and fry 1 tbsp chopped fresh ginger, 1 tsp chopped chilli and 1 tsp chopped garlic until fragrant, then mix through the soup, seasoning with soy sauce, for an Asian-flavoured winner.

Vegetable and bean chilli with three-cheese quesadillas

Don't be put off by the long list of ingredients – you probably have a lot of these in your cupboard or fridge already – and the spices really do lift this chilli out of the realms of the ordinary to the exotic. And if you haven't got these specific beans, be bold and just swap in the ones you do have. Using three types of cheese in the quesadillas might seem excessive but again it's just taking a concept that can be quite subtle and giving it tang and bang. Use what you have if you don't want to go for all three.

Serves 4–6

Chilli

2 tbsp rapeseed oil
2 small cinnamon sticks
1 large carrot, grated
2 celery sticks, cut into small dice
2 red onions, finely chopped
6 garlic cloves, crushed
2 red bird's eye chillies, chopped (with or without seeds, depending on how hot you want your chilli)
3 tbsp tomato purée
2 bay leaves
3 tsp ground cumin
2 tsp ground coriander
1 tsp smoked paprika
2 tsp chopped thyme
400g tin chopped tomatoes
1 red pepper, finely diced
1 yellow pepper, finely diced
1 x 400g tin kidney beans, drained
1 x 400g tin chickpeas, drained
1 x 400g tin black-eye beans, drained
30g coriander, chopped

1 Put the oil in a heavy-based pan over a high heat and fry the cinnamon stick until fragrant. Add the carrot, celery, onion, garlic and chilli and sweat until the onions are translucent – about 10 minutes. Add the tomato purée and stir for 30 seconds, then add the bay leaves, ground cumin and coriander, smoked paprika and thyme and stir-fry for a minute. Pour in the chopped tomatoes, and simmer for 15 minutes, stirring occasionally, then add the peppers and simmer for 10 minutes until they are just cooked through. Add all the beans, stir, bring back to a simmer, cover and cook on low heat for 10–15 minutes. Add the coriander leaves and season.

Quesadillas
100g Cheddar, grated
100g Gruyère cheese, grated
100g Manchego cheese, grated
100g spring onions, sliced
oil for frying
6 tortilla wraps
salt and pepper
sour cream, to serve

2 To make the quesadillas, mix the three cheeses with the spring onions in a bowl. Heat a large heavy frying pan over a medium heat and brush the pan with oil. Place a wrap in the pan and sprinkle a third of the cheese mix over it evenly. Cook for 1 minute, then top with another wrap, pressing down the edges, and cook till the bottom wrap is golden brown and crispy. Flip over and cook until the other side is also golden. Take the quesadilla off the pan, cut into three and repeat to make two more quesadillas. Serve the quesadillas with the chilli and a bowl of sour cream.

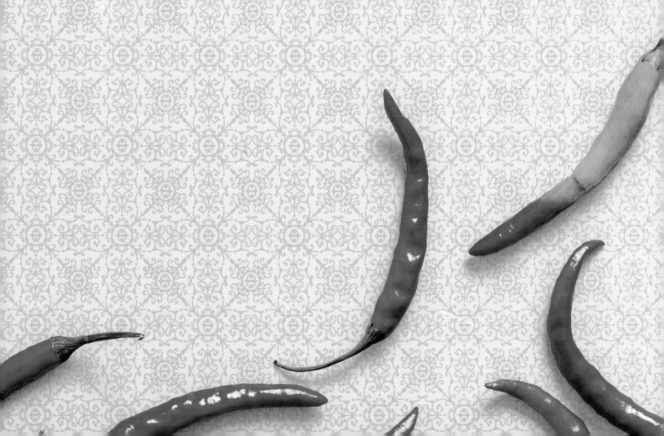

Oooh err, quiche

Quiche was always a bit of a joke if you grew up in the 1970s. It was normally soggy and insipid with a cold, eggy filling. Made properly, with crisp, buttery pastry and a rich tasty custard, quiche is great. The classic – quiche Lorraine – is hard to beat; the saltiness of the bacon combined with cheese and soft herbs just comes together beautifully. Here I've given you several different options.

Serves 4–6

Pastry
175g plain flour
75g chilled unsalted butter, cut into
  cubes
good pinch of salt
1 tbsp cold water
1 egg, beaten

Custard
300g whipping or single cream
4 eggs (plus the excess beaten egg
  from making the pastry)
freshly ground black pepper

1. Preheat the oven to 200°C/gas 6. Grease a 22cm loose-bottomed, fluted flan tin.

2. Start with the pastry. In a bowl, mix the flour, butter and salt with your fingertips until the mixture resembles breadcrumbs. Make a well in the middle and add the water and 1 tablespoon of the beaten egg (add the rest to the filling). Mix until a dough forms, then pat into a round, wrap in cling film and leave to rest in the fridge for 30 minutes.

3. Lightly dust a work surface and roll out the pastry until it is roughly 3mm thick (like a pound coin). Line the flan tin with the pastry, easing it into the base. Trim the pastry edges (save any trimmings) so it sits slightly above the tin. Press the pastry into the flutes, lightly prick the base with a fork, then chill for 10 minutes.

4. Line the pastry case with greaseproof paper, fill with dry beans and bake for 20 minutes. Remove the paper and beans and bake for an additional 4-5 minutes, until the pastry is pale golden. If you notice any small holes or cracks, patch them up with pastry trimmings.

5. Now you can make any kind of quiche (see fillings opposite).

6. Place a baking sheet in the oven to heat. Make the custard. Whisk the cream and eggs (including the extra beaten egg from the pastry) in a bowl, season well and transfer to a jug. Add your chosen filling (see opposite) to the pastry case. (If you're making the quiche Lorraine, just scatter over the bacon.)

7. Half-pull the oven shelf out and put the flan tin on the baking sheet. Quickly pour the custard into the pastry case – you get it right to the top this way – and scatter over the cheeses if making quiche Lorraine, then carefully push the shelf back into the oven. Lower the oven to 190°C/gas 5. Bake the quiche for about 25 minutes, or until golden and softly set (the centre should not feel too firm). Let the quiche settle for 4–5 minutes, then remove from the tin. Serve freshly baked, although it's also good cold.

Stilton and celery with chilli jam

150g Chilli Jam (see page 246),
red onion marmalade
or shop-bought chutney
175g Stilton, grated
100g celery, trimmed and finely sliced
1 tbsp chopped flat-leaf parsley

Spread the chilli jam over the pastry case then scatter over the Stilton, celery and parsley and continue as directed in the recipe.

Smoked salmon and crowdie cheese

200g smoked salmon, cut into ribbons
200g crowdie cheese (see page 221) or cream cheese
1 tsp chopped dill

Arrange the smoked salmon over the pastry case, dot over the cheese then scatter over the dill and continue as directed in the recipe..

Lorraine

175g dry-cured streaky bacon,
fried till crispy, then drained on kitchen paper and cooled
75g Cheddar cheese, grated
(I like Isle of Mull)
75g Gruyère cheese, grated

Add the ingredients to the pastry case as directed in the recipe.

Smoky chorizo

1 tbsp vegetable oil
1 shallot, sliced
1 garlic clove, finely chopped
½ tsp smoked paprika
150g chorizo, chopped
roasted red peppers from a jar, cut into strips
½ x 400g tin chopped tomatoes
1 tbsp caster sugar
1 tbsp sherry vinegar
100g grated manchego
salt and pepper

Heat the oil in a heavy-bottomed pan. Add the shallot and garlic and fry for 5 minutes, then add the paprika and chorizo and cook for another 5 minutes. Add the peppers and tomatoes and cook for 5 minutes more, then add the sugar and vinegar and cook for 10 minutes. Season to taste. Cool then add to the pastry case, along with the cheese.

Baked sweet potato curry

This is a cheap and cheerful recipe. I have baked the sweet potato so it keeps its delicate sweet flavour but if you don't have time for that just pop the raw potato in when directed and you can cook it in the curry. I've included a tin of chickpeas for extra bulk but you can leave it out if you wish.

Serves 4–6

750g sweet potato, left whole if
    baking; cut into bite-sized cubes
    if cooking in the curry
1 tbsp rapeseed oil
1 tbsp cumin seeds
1 onion, finely sliced
salt and pepper
2 garlic cloves, crushed
½ tsp chilli powder
½ tsp garam masala
60g ginger, peeled and grated
1 x 400g tin chickpeas, drained
250g tinned tomatoes

1. If you are baking your potatoes (see above), preheat the oven to 180°C/gas 4.

2. Place the potatoes on a baking sheet and bake for 20 minutes (you want the potato just under cooked so it's still firm). Leave to cool and cut into bite-sized chunks.

3. Heat a large saucepan over a medium heat and add the oil. When it's hot, add the cumin seeds and fry until aromatic. Add the onion and a pinch of salt and cook for 5–6 minutes, or until the onion is soft and translucent. Add the garlic, chilli, garam masala and ginger and fry for a further 2–3 minutes.

4. Add the chickpeas, tomatoes, and three quarters of a tin of water. Add the raw sweet potato pieces (if you are not baking the sweet potato first). Cover with a lid and simmer over a medium–low heat, stirring now and again, for 30 minutes, or until the sauce has thickened and the chickpeas are tender. Stir in the baked sweet potato (if using) and bring back to a boil. Taste the curry and season to taste with salt and pepper. Serve immediately.

Chickpea burger with smoked aubergine and grilled ciabatta

This is one for veggies who, like me, have burger envy It's our chance to hold a big bun in our hands and chow down on a hearty filling, with great texture and loads of flavour. Burger-tastic..

Serves 6

200g dried chickpeas
150g tinned chickpeas (drained weight
  – you'll need a 400g tin)
1 small red onion, peeled and roughly
  chopped
6 garlic cloves, peeled
zest of 2 lemons and juice of ½
2 tsp ground cumin
1 tsp ground coriander
½ tsp chilli powder
¼ tsp ground cardamom
70g coriander (leaves and stalks),
  roughly chopped
20g parsley leaves
10g tarragon leaves
1½ tsp salt
½ tsp bicarbonate of soda
2 tbsp gram flour (if needed)
vegetable oil, for frying
4 ciabatta rolls
1 batch of Aubergine Filling
  (see page 141), to serve

1 Put the dried chickpeas in bowl or a pot that will take the beans plus six times their quantity of water (the beans will triple in volume when soaked). Soak for 24 hours then drain well.

2 Place both types of chickpeas in a food processor with the onion, garlic, lemon zest and juice, all the spices and herbs, salt and baking soda. Pulse until all the herbs are chopped and mixed with the other ingredients – it should be a thick semi-smooth green paste: you are after a firm mix that you can mould into balls with damp hands. If the mixture is too wet, add the gram flour. Taste and adjust the seasoning.

3 Heat 5cm of vegetable oil in a frying pan. Shape four to six burgers from the mixture with lightly oiled hands and fry them in batches for 4–5 minutes on each side, until golden brown. Place on an oiled tray in a low oven to keep warm while you cook the rest.

4 Heat a griddle pan over a medium heat, then toast the ciabatta halves until you have nice char marks. Pile the aubergine – either hot or cold (it's great either way) – on to the bottom halves, add a hot burger, top with the lids and serve.

Falafel with Satan's ketchup

Until I tried proper falafels in Egypt, I never understood what all the fuss was about. Then I had them fresh at a stall and I got it! The vendor was good enough to give me his recipe and here it is. Two tips he gave me: the less water added to the mix, the better, as there's less chance of the falafel breaking up in the oil. And secondly, you must make sure the oil for frying is nice and hot – set at 160°C. The Satan's ketchup is the other wee gem here: tomato ketchup given a good kick with garlic and chilli. This is a mild version of what I usually have – if you want the full kick, double the amount of garlic and chilli.

Serves 4–6

250g dried chickpeas
2 small red onions, roughly chopped
100g coriander, leaves and stalks roughly chopped
50g flat-leaf parsley leaves
50g tarragon leaves
6 garlic cloves, peeled
2 tsp salt
2 tsp ground cumin
1 tsp pepper
1 tsp ground coriander
½ tsp baking soda
½ tsp chilli powder
¼ tsp ground cardamom
juice and zest of 1 lemon
about 3 tbsp gram flour

Satan's ketchup

3 tbsp rapeseed oil
1 small onion, finely chopped
6 garlic cloves, crushed
8 hot green chillies, roughly chopped
2–3 tbsp vinegar
1 large bottle of tomato ketchup
  of your choice – about 650ml
salt and pepper
sugar, to taste

1 Put the chickpeas in a bowl or a pot that will hold them with at least six times the quantity of water. Cover with cold water – loads of cold water – as the chickpeas will triple in volume. Soak for 24 hours.

2 To make the ketchup, heat the oil in a pan and sweat the onions and garlic for 5 minutes without colouring. Turn up the heat and keep stirring. When the onions and garlic start to colour, add the chillies and fry for 2 minutes. Take off the heat and stir in 2 tablespoons of the vinegar, making sure to dislodge any bits stuck to the bottom of the pan. Transfer the mixture to a blender, and add the tomato ketchup and some salt and pepper. Whizz, then taste and adjust with sugar and more salt, pepper and vinegar, as needed.

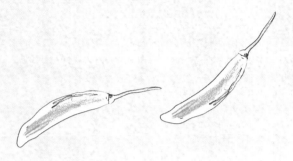

3 Drain the chickpeas well and reserve the soaking water in case you need to wet the mixture. Put the chickpeas in a food processor and pulse until the texture is similar to fine breadcrumbs. Remember to scrape down the sides of bowl. Add the remaining ingredients (except for the gram flour) and pulse until mixed. You are after a firm mix that you can mould into balls with damp hands. If the mixture is too dry, add a spoonful of soaking water; if it is too wet, add gram flour, a tablespoon at a time. Taste and adjust the seasoning.

4 Mould the mixture into balls slightly smaller in size than a golf ball (about 1 tbsp per ball). Pop them on a lightly oiled tray and continue shaping balls until the mix is all used up.

5 Put a deep-fat fryer on to 160°C or fill a deep pan a quarter full with oil and heat. Fry the falafel in batches of six at a time for 4–5 minutes, until golden brown. Drain on kitchen paper. Serve warm or cooled to room temperature with the Satan's ketchup.

Artichoke risotto cakes, kohlrabi and spring onion salad with red wine dressing

This dish is a two-in-one. Make it as risotto if you want, or carry on and make the risotto cakes. You won't need the full amount of dressing but you can just pop any left over in a clean jar – it will happily sit in the fridge for a few weeks.

Serves 6–8

Risotto

1.5 litres vegetable stock
2 tbsp extra virgin olive oil
50g butter
2 brown onions, finely chopped
4 garlic cloves, crushed
600g arborio rice
250ml dry white wine
12 marinated baby artichokes, chopped into bite-sized pieces
80g finely grated Parmesan
1 tbsp chopped flat-leaf parsley
2 tsp chopped tarragon
salt and pepper
lemon wedges, to serve (optional)

For making risotto cakes

1 egg, lightly beaten
200g dried breadcrumbs
50g grated Parmesan
vegetable oil, for frying
salt and pepper

Kohlrabi and spring onion salad

1 large kohlrabi (or celeriac if it's hard to find)
2 eating apples
1 batch of Red Wine Dressing (see page 247)
salt and pepper

1 Bring the stock to a simmer. Reduce the heat to low and keep it at a gentle simmer.

2 Heat the oil and butter in a large saucepan over a medium heat until the butter melts. Add the onion and garlic and cook, stirring, for 5 minutes, or until the onion softens without colouring.

3 Add the rice and cook, stirring, for 2 minutes, or until the rice grains appear glassy and coated in butter. Add the wine and cook, stirring constantly, for 5 minutes, or until all the liquid is absorbed. Add the stock, one ladleful at a time, stirring continuously and waiting until all the liquid is absorbed before adding more. Cook for 20–25 minutes, or until the rice is tender yet firm to the bite and the risotto is creamy. Remove from the heat.

4 Add the artichokes, Parmesan and herbs and stir to combine. Taste and season with salt and pepper.

5 Either serve straight away with a drizzle of olive oil and a wedge of lemon or to make the cakes...

6 Pour the risotto on to a tray, cover with cling film and leave to cool completely. Transfer to the fridge for 2–4 hours to firm up.

7 Meanwhile, prepare the salad. Peel the kohlrabi, cut in half and slice thinly, then shred the slices into matchsticks. Core the apples and slice to the same thickness and size as the kohlrabi. Mix in a large bowl, then add enough dressing to suit your tastes, and mix well.

8 Form the mixture into eight cakes. Put the beaten egg into a shallow dish. Mix the breadcrumbs and Parmesan in another.

9 Dip the cakes into the egg then into the breadcrumbs, coating thoroughly. Pour 1 tablespoon of oil into a large heavy-based frying pan. Heat over a medium–high heat. Working in batches, fry the risotto cakes until crisp and brown, about 2 minutes per side. Serve the cakes with the dressed salad on the side.

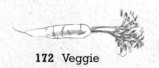

Nasi goreng pattaya

This is a wonderful way to use up what's in the fridge but it's a bit showy at the same time. I was given this as staff food one day in my old restaurant Oloroso. Nick from Singapore was on the stove that day and explained that it's basically fried rice with whatever you have in the fridge, spiced and served, usually, with cucumber and tomatoes, and of course, with chilli sauce. Here I've made it with mushrooms, but if you're not cooking for vegetarians you could replace these with leftover Beef Brisket (see page 33), Pork Shoulder (see page 60) or Peanut Butter Chicken Thighs (see page 75), or indeed anything else that you want to use up.

Serves 4

vegetable oil
4 garlic cloves, crushed
2.5cm piece of fresh ginger, peeled
   and chopped
4 shallots, finely chopped
1 red Serrano chilli, finely chopped
1 tsp garam masala
1 tsp vegetable stock powder
   (I use Marigold bouillon powder)
100g white cabbage, finely sliced
   and washed
a handful of mushrooms (or see the
   introduction)
400g cold cooked rice
100g frozen petit pois
2 tbsp chopped coriander
8 eggs
salt and pepper
chilli sauce, to serve

1 Heat 2 tablespoons of oil in a wok over a high heat. Add the garlic and ginger and stir-fry for 1 minute. Add the shallots and chilli and cook for 1 minute. Add the garam masala, bouillon powder, cabbage and mushrooms. Cover with a lid and cook for 2 minutes (there should be enough water on the cabbage to steam it so that everything cooks with out sticking). Add the rice and keep moving it about till broken up and hot, then stir in the petit pois and leave for 1 minute. Scrape the mixture into a bowl and stir in the coriander. Leave aside while you make the omelettes.

2 Heat a large non-stick frying pan for the omelettes. In a small bowl, beat 2 of the eggs very well with a pinch of salt. Add to the pan and swirl it around to make a very thin omelette. When the omelette is almost cooked through, remove and transfer to a large plate. Repeat with the remaining omelette mixture. Gently reheat the rice mixture over a very low heat, or ideally reheat single portions in a microwave. Add one portion of fried rice to one half of each omelette and carefully fold it over. Slide on to a plate and serve with chilli sauce.

Humungous onion rings

Okay, you can get onion rings, you can get large onion rings and now you can have humungous onion rings. It was in America that I first tried these, although there they were served battered and were a bit too greasy for you to eat more than one. I thought they were such a great idea that I decided to tweak the concept and fry them in breadcrumbs for a semi-healthier treat. The hardest part is getting onions big enough for huge rings. Go for British brown onions but if you want even bigger rings, try to find Spanish.

Serves 4

vegetable oil, for deep-frying
2 large onions
250g plain flour
salt
2 eggs
200ml milk
250g dried breadcrumbs
Spice Mix (see page 248)

Chef's tip

You can also fill these to make them a little more substantial. I stuff mine with the Baked Sweet Potato Curry (see page 167), the Vegetable and Bean Chilli (see page 160) or even some salad for a bit of freshness.

1. Put a deep-fat fryer on to 185°C or fill a deep pan a quarter full with oil and heat.

2. Peel the onions, trim off the root and the top, then cut them in half crossways. Separate the onion slices into rings. Soak in water for a couple of hours if you can.

3. In a shallow dish, stir together the flour and a good pinch of salt. In another bowl whisk the eggs and milk. Put the breadcrumbs into a third shallow dish.

4. Dip the onion rings in the flour, then the egg, then the breadcrumbs until they are all coated. Scoop the crumbs up over each ring to coat. Give each ring a hard tap as you remove it from the crumbs – the coating should cling very well.

5. Deep-fry the rings three at a time for 2–3 minutes, or until golden brown. Remove to kitchen paper to drain. Season with salt and the spice mix and serve at once, or see the chef's tip below.

05 SHORT AND SWEET

Both my heritages celebrate good food, good cheer and a love of the sweeter things in life. Show a Scottish Sikh a menu and the first thing they will look at will be the puddings! And I am no exception; I absolutely love all things sweet and sticky, chocolatey and spongy. From fine Scottish baking and sweet-making (tablet is nothing short of ambrosia to me) to the Indian love of sweetmeats (my personal food equivalent of kryptonite), I've always been surrounded by sugary goodness. So in this chapter you'll discover lots of sweet, creamy, hot and icy indulgences.

These puddings are some of my favourites. There are two trifles, because quite frankly, who doesn't love discovering the many layers of a trifle with their different flavours and textures; a rice pudding, which for me is without question a dish to love, hot or cold; together with traditional baked puds, like the cobbler, which takes me back to my college days, and an Arctic roll – the cutting edge of cool when I was a lad. Then there are puds that are just sheer indulgence: I suggest you turn immediately to page 224 to discover the wonder that is my Nutella pancake gateau. Enough said; my mouth is watering at the thought.

Not even I indulge in pudding every day but as a treat they truly are wonderful.

Chocolate shortbread trifle

My kids told me I had to put a shortbread recipe in the book; they know my weakness for it. I'm quite a dab hand at shortbread and it has to be just right: super short – so crisp it could shatter – but also melt-in-the-mouth buttery, and baked without colour – it should be a lovely blonde, like the sands around Scotland. But I've gone a bit off-piste here as this trifle has chocolate shortbread in it – definitely not blonde but super tasty.

Serves 10

4 oranges
25ml Grand Marnier (optional)
200g thick custard
300g whipping cream
chocolate shavings, to decorate

Chocolate shortbread

110g caster sugar
60g icing sugar
1 tsp salt
80g cocoa powder
340g butter, chilled
    and cut into small cubes
410g plain flour

1 Preheat the oven to 160°C/gas 3 and line a baking tray with greaseproof paper.

2 Firstly make the shortbread. Sift together all the dry ingredients except the flour. Rub in the butter to give a breadcrumb texture, then gradually add the flour to form a dough.

3 Shape the dough into two logs each approximately 5cm in diameter and chill for 20 minutes.

4 Cut the logs into 1.5cm slices and place on the lined baking tray. Bake in the oven for 12 minutes, then take out and leave to cool.

5 Grate the zest of two of the oranges and set aside. Remove the skins from all four oranges and segment them, leaving behind any white pith. Divide the orange segments between 10 glass tumblers and add a splash of Grand Marnier if desired. Spoon in some of the thick custard and sprinkle with the orange zest. Break up pieces of the chocolate shortbread and scatter on top of the custard.

6 Finally, whip the cream until the whisk leaves a ribbon trail when lifted (semi-whipped). Cover the trifles and decorate with the chocolate shavings.

Pineapple rice pudding

This is a very traditional vanilla rice pudding mixture but I'm serving it with pineapple that has been cooked in a very mildly spiced sugar syrup. The fruit cuts through the rich pudding and gives it a nice light, crunchy lift that contrasts with the silky creaminess.

Serves 4

Rice pudding
200g pudding rice
500ml milk
½ x 400g tin condensed milk
1 tsp vanilla extract
10g caster sugar

Pineapple topping
150g caster sugar
150ml water
1 star anise
1 vanilla pod, split in half, seeds
  scraped out
1 pineapple, skin removed, cored and
  diced

1 For the pineapple, place the sugar, water, star anise, vanilla pod and seeds in a pan. Bring to the boil then immediately remove from the heat. Add the pineapple to the syrup, place back on the heat and bring to a simmer, then take off and allow to cool.

2 Place all the rice pudding ingredients in a pan and cook on a medium heat for about 45 minutes, until soft and creamy, stirring all the time.

3 To serve, ladle the pudding into bowls, make a well in the centre of each and scoop in lots of the pineapple.

Chocolate Arctic roll

A totally retro dessert. It was a lawyer who came up with the idea of wrapping vanilla ice cream in a thin layer of sponge in the 1950s and suddenly it was being served on dining tables throughout the '60s and '70s. Sadly, the practice of making it at home eventually went out of fashion – it became a bit tacky, but I'm a big fan and would love to see a revival of this classic pud. This is a bit of a posh version, I'll admit – a chocolate sponge with a decadent praline filling made from Nutella, and chopped hazelnuts for some lovely crunch. It might seem like a bit of a faff to make but I promise you, one bite and you won't doubt it was worth it.

Serves 6–8

Praline parfait filling
4 egg yolks and 3 egg whites
45g caster sugar
200ml double cream
75g Nutella hazelnut spread
75g peeled hazelnuts, chopped

Swiss roll
40g plain flour
30g cocoa powder
6 eggs (3 whole, 3 separated)
110g caster sugar
45g soft light brown sugar
200g Nutella hazelnut spread

To serve
Custard, cream or jelly

1. Start by making the praline filling. In an electric mixer or using a hand whisk, whisk the egg yolks and half the sugar until very pale yellow, almost white, in colour. This will take about 10 minutes.

2. In another spotlessly clean bowl, whisk the egg whites to stiff peaks (the bowl and whisk need to be free of grease otherwise the egg white will not incorporate air). Slowly whisk in the other half of the sugar until stiff. You'll know it's ready because you'll be able to hold the bowl over your head. If it stays in the bowl, it's ready; if not, clean up the mess and tell no one.

3. In another bowl, whip the cream and Nutella until when you lift the whisk you leave a ribbon trail (semi-whipped).

4. Gently fold the egg yolk mixture into the cream. Stir a third of the beaten egg whites into the cream mixture. Fold in the remainder, then add the chopped nuts, being very careful not to lose too much volume.

5. Pour the mixture into a 23 x 33cm Swiss roll tin and put in the freezer until set. Depending on your freezer, this will take at least 4 hours, but overnight is best.

6. Meanwhile, make the Swiss roll. Preheat the oven to 210°C/gas 6½. Line a second 23 x 33cm Swiss roll tin with greaseproof paper.

Note
You will need two Swiss roll
tins to make this recipe.

7 Sift the flour and cocoa powder into a bowl. Take the three eggs and three yolks, place in a mixing bowl with the caster sugar and whisk until pale and doubled in volume.

8 Whisk the 3 egg whites with the brown sugar until soft peaks form, then carefully fold this into the egg yolk mixture. Finally, gently fold in the sifted flour and cocoa powder.

9 Pour the batter into the lined tin and spread out evenly. Bake for about 10–15 minutes then carefully lift out of the tin, remove the paper and place on a clean tea towel. Once the sponge is cool, warm the Nutella. You can either place the jar in a pan of just-boiled water (off the heat) for 10 minutes or transfer it to a bowl and microwave for 30 seconds on high, until soft. Carefully spread the warm Nutella over the sponge (don't tear it).

10 To assemble the roll, take the parfait out the freezer and trim it so it is just a bit smaller than the sponge then place the parfait on top of the roll. Using the tea towel to help you, roll up the sponge firmly and tightly. Once rolled, put on a tray and cover with cling film. Place in the freezer until you are ready to serve. Slice with a hot knife and serve with custard, cream or jelly or whatever you fancy.

Berry jelly, oat crunch and whisky cream cheese

This is a great summer recipe for when you have an abundance of soft fruit that you don't know what to do with. You can use fresh berries or frozen ones, either shop-bought or ones you've frozen yourself for later in the year, as I did here.

Serves 6

1kg berries (use any berries of your choice), fresh or frozen
100g granulated sugar
a few gelatine leaves (see method)
50g clear honey
50g unsalted butter
150g rolled oats
100–120g icing sugar
500g cream cheese, at room temperature
40ml good-quality blended Scottish whisky (I use Whyte and McKay)

1 Place the berries and sugar in a large pan over a low–medium heat and allow to soften slowly. Once soft, strain the berries, return the juice to the pan and bubble to reduce by a third. Measure the quantity of hot berry juice: you will need one gelatine leaf per 100ml of juice. Soak the appropriate number of gelatin leaves in cold water.

2 Once softened, drain, squeeze out any excess water, add to the hot berry liquid and dissolve fully.

3 Spoon some of the berries into fat tumblers or glasses, pour in the warm berry jelly mix and chill for at least 2 hours until set.

4 Preheat the oven to 160°C/gas 3. Place the honey and butter in a pan, bring to the boil and stir in the oats. Transfer to a lined baking tray and bake for how about 15–20 minutes or until golden.

5 Allow to cool then break up into small pieces. Sprinkle on top of the set jelly.

6 Sift the icing sugar into the cream cheese and stir in as much of the whisky as desired. Spoon this mixture on top of the crunchy oats. Sprinkle over some more oats and/or berries and serve.

Pumpkin empanadas with dulche de leche

Pumpkin in a pudding? I was sceptical, but I tried these in New York when I was there promoting 'Tartan Week' for Visit Scotland. I ate some cool stuff that week – pumpkin pie that was totally awesome, and empanadas with all kinds of fillings – sweet, savoury and everything in between. The word 'empanada', meaning 'in pastry', makes these sound exotic, but just think of them as small sweet Cornish pasties. Dulce de leche is an Argentinian caramel cream – super sweet but super tasty and the result is a filling not dissimilar to a pumpkin pie.

Makes 12

1 x 400g tin condensed milk
550g peeled pumpkin, cut into
   2.5cm dice
4 tsp vegetable oil
40g soft light brown sugar
nutmeg, freshly grated
ice cream, to serve

Pastry
170g plain flour
50g caster sugar
½ tsp salt
½ tsp ground cinnamon
100g unsalted butter, from the fridge
1 egg yolk
20ml cold water
1 egg, beaten

To save time...
Dulce de leche is now widely available to buy ready-made. You'll find 450g jars in most supermarkets so pop one of those in your trolley and skip the 3 hours' boiling stage.

1   Preheat the oven to 160°C/gas 3.

2   For the dulce de leche, place the unopened tin of condensed milk in a pan, cover with water and simmer gently for 3 hours, topping up the water when necessary to ensure the tin is always kept covered with water to prevent the risk of it exploding. Remove and leave to cool.

3   Place the diced pumpkin on a baking tray and sprinkle with the oil, brown sugar and some freshly grated nutmeg. Bake in the oven for about 45 minutes, until slightly softened. Keep an eye on it to make sure it doesn't start to caramelise or blacken around the edges. Mash the cooked pumpkin and set aside to cool.

4   For the pastry, sift the flour, sugar, salt and cinnamon into a bowl. Cut the butter into small pieces and rub it into the dry ingredients until you have a breadcrumb texture. Add the egg yolk and the water and bring it together to form a dough. Wrap in cling film and leave to rest for 1 hour in the fridge.

5   Roll out the pastry on a floured surface to a thickness of 5mm. Cut out discs of the pastry about 10cm across, using a small side plate as a template.

6   Place a large spoonful of the pumpkin filling in the centre of each pastry disc, and place a spoonful of the dulce de leche on top. Brush the beaten egg around the edge of the pastry and draw up the sides, encasing the filling (it should look like a mini Cornish pasty). Crimp the edges together between your fingertips.

7   Place the empanadas on a tray lined with greaseproof paper and brush them all over with beaten egg. Bake in the oven for 10–12 minutes, until golden brown all over. Serve with ice cream.

Pear and peach Charlotte

This Charlotte is a show-stopping dessert yet deceptively simple to fling together.
There's no shame in buying your Swiss roll rather than making your own – it cuts
the time and there are some really good brands available now.

Serves 6–8

200g caster sugar
200ml water
2 ripe peaches, stoned and chopped
   into small dice
50g butter
2 ripe pears, peeled and cored
200–300g whipping cream
40g icing sugar
2 good-quality Swiss rolls, thinly sliced

1. Line a 900g plastic pudding basin or similar-sized bowl with cling film.

2. Combine the sugar and water in a pan and bring it to the boil, then simmer for 3 minutes or until syrupy. Remove from the heat.

3. Cook the peaches gently in 25g butter until softened – about 5 minutes – then set aside to cool.

4. Slice the pears into thin wedges and cook very gently in the remaining 25g butter until just soft – again, about 5 minutes, then leave to cool.

5. Whip the cream with the icing sugar until when you lift the whisk it leaves a ribbon trail (semi-whipped).

6. Line the pudding basin with Swiss roll slices and moisten them by brushing with some of the sugar syrup. Cover the slices with a thin layer of the whipped cream. Place a layer of the peaches over the base of the pudding, followed by a bit more cream. Lay more Swiss roll slices on top of the cream and follow this with a layer of the pears. Finish with the remainder of the Swiss roll slices (any leftover cream can be used for serving).

7. Cover with more cling film and weigh down lightly with a side plate or something that fits well and a tin of beans. Chill for 4–5 hours.

8. To serve, carefully turn the Charlotte out on to a serving plate, remove the cling film and slice. Serve with leftover whipped cream.

Pippin apple and honey cobbler with custard

Both Americans and Brits make cobblers – a pudding that's not a million miles away from a crumble. In the UK, traditional cobblers were savoury: some kind of scone topping was placed on a stew-like filling, like cobbles. This one is most definitely the American variety, which is always made with fruit and a light batter on the top that will crisp up and add crunch – it's more like a biscuit. It's said that cobblers were brought to the States by the early British settlers; they couldn't get hold of suet to make their pie or pudding crusts, so the resourceful bakers improvised and tried to recreate their beloved puds as best they could. This cobbler can be made with any fruit in any season but I think this lovely light apple version makes a great end to Sunday lunch.

Serves 4–6

200g clear honey
zest of 1 lemon
1 cinnamon stick
1kg Cox's Orange Pippin apples, peeled, cored and chopped into 2cm dice
300g plain flour
1½ tbsp baking powder
1 tsp salt
125g milk
125g caster sugar
110g unsalted butter
fresh custard, to serve

1 Preheat the oven to 150°C/gas 2.

2 Place the honey in a pan. Add the lemon zest and cinnamon stick and boil for 2 minutes. Add the apples and cook until just softened. Once cooked, strain the apples, place the liquid back in the pan and boil until reduced to a syrup – this will take about 5 minutes.

3 For the cobbler topping, sift the flour, baking powder and salt into a bowl. Heat the milk in a pan, then add the sugar and butter and stir to dissolve. Pour this into the dry mixture and stir to form a batter.

4 Place the apple mixture in a 20 x 25cm pie dish. Pour over the reduced honey syrup and mix gently. Spoon over the cobbler topping and flatten with a wetted palette knife or spatula.

5 Bake in the oven for 30–40 minutes until risen and golden brown. Serve with custard.

Parkin and blue cheese

I was given this recipe by my auntie Anjali who was from Leeds but moved up to Edinburgh when she got married. It was the first time I had something that my 'Asian' auntie had baked. I was quite surprised: I thought she only knew how to make Indian food, but her parkin was lovely – moist and tasty. It's great with blue cheese on top or you can dip it in my Blue cheese sauce (see page 252). You can also use this parkin in the Gingerbread Pudding recipe (see page 211).

Serves 6–8

225g plain flour
2 tsp salt
2½ tsp baking powder
2 tsp ground ginger
55g unsalted butter, diced
55g lard, diced
225g oatmeal
115g soft light brown sugar
170g treacle
170g golden syrup
60ml milk
250g creamy blue cheese, such as
  Dolcelatte or cambozola, to serve

1. Preheat the oven to 170°C/ gas 5½. Line a deep 40 x 30cm tray with greaseproof paper.

2. Sift the flour, salt, baking powder and ginger together into a large bowl. Add the diced fats and rub to a breadcrumb consistency. Mix in the oatmeal and the sugar.

3. Warm the treacle, golden syrup and milk in a pan. Pour into the flour mixture and mix well.

4. Pour the mixture into the prepared baking tray and bake in the oven for about 40 minutes. Insert a skewer into the centre of the cake. If it comes out clean, it's ready; if not, bake for a further 5 minutes.

5. Allow the parkin to cool slightly before slicing. Serve with slices of creamy blue cheese. However, if you can keep your hands off it long enough, it will taste even better a week later – keep it in a cake tin and it will get all sticky and moist.

Baked Alaska

Baked Alaska has a wow factor and it's very simple to do if you bend the rules and buy some of the component parts. I suggest you buy the Madeira cake, ice cream or sorbet and then make the meringue yourself. Simple. Then you bring it out, pour on the warm alcohol and flambé.

Serves 4

50g marmalade (I like thin-cut but you can use whichever type you prefer)
4 slices shop-bought lemon Madeira cake (I often use a cutter to get nice even rounds)
1 orange
1 ruby grapefruit
4 scoops good-quality berry sorbet
3 tbsp Grand Marnier (optional)

Meringue
350g caster sugar
75g water
185g egg whites (about 4–5 medium eggs)

Note
You will need a sugar thermometer for this recipe.

1. Start by making the meringue. Place the sugar and water into a pan and heat to 121°C (use a sugar thermometer). When the sugar reaches the required temperature, start to whisk the egg whites in a freestanding mixer or with an electric hand whisk. Once they start to get frothy, slowly add the sugar mixture down the side of the bowl (be careful not to let it touch the whisk as this will spin all the syrup round the bowl and not into the meringue). Keep whisking until cool (about 10 minutes) then transfer to a piping bag fitted with a star nozzle to finish cooling.

2. To assemble the Alaska, cut four pieces of greaseproof paper about 12cm square and place them on a baking tray. Spread the marmalade over one side of each of the cake slices, then place these in the centre of the paper squares.

3. Next, peel the oranges and grapefruit, removing as much pith as possible, then cut them into segments by cutting between each layer of membrane. Lay the segments (you'll need about eight of each) around the cake slices in an overlapping fan style, leaving a space between the segment tips in the middle for the sorbet. Place a scoop of sorbet in the centre of the fruit.

4. Finally, pipe the meringue in spikes all over the cake, fruit and sorbet so it looks like a hedgehog. Pop it straight into the freezer for 3–4 hours

5. Preheat the oven to 240°C/gas 9.

6. Bake the Alaskas for 3 minutes, until the peaks are golden (watch them carefully as they burn easily). Meanwhile, gently heat the Grand Marnier, if using.

7. Remove the Alaskas from the oven and serve immediately. For a final dash of drama, pour the warm Grand Marnier over each pud and carefully set light to it with a match.

Passion fruit and mascarpone trifle with amaretti crumbs

It's trifle Jim, but not as you know it.

Serves 4–6, depending on the size of your glasses

Jelly
3½ leaves of gelatine
125g caster sugar
375g passion fruit juice
juice of 2 large oranges

Custard
400g milk
100g double cream
4 egg yolks
100g sugar
10g custard powder
few drops of vanilla extract

Mascarpone topping
300g double cream
50g caster sugar
5g vanilla extract
300g mascarpone
amaretti biscuits, crushed
    (you'll need about 3 per serving),

1. Soak the gelatine leaves in cold water until soft, then squeeze out any excess water.

2. Meanwhile, place the sugar and fruit juices in a pan and heat until the sugar has dissolved. Take off the heat, add the gelatine and stir until dissolved, then pour into glasses – I generally use short tumblers – and place in the fridge for 2 hours to set.

3. For the custard, place the milk and cream in a pan and bring to the boil then immediately turn off the heat.

4. Meanwhile mix the egg yolks, sugar, custard powder and vanilla extract together. Gradually pour the warm milk over the yolk mixture, whisking continuously.

5. Pour the mixture into a clean pan and place over a medium heat. Bring to the boil then reduce the heat and simmer for 5 minutes until the custard is thick and creamy. Remove from the heat, cover with greaseproof paper and allow to cool before pouring a thin layer on to the jelly made earlier (any leftover custard isn't going to go to waste, I'm sure!).

6. For the mascarpone topping, place the cream, sugar and vanilla extract into a bowl and whip to form soft peaks. Fold in the mascarpone. Pipe or spoon on top of the custard and finish by sprinkling over the crushed amaretti biscuits.

Chocolate samosas with 5 fillings

Samosas surprise people with how easy they are to make and also how many different sorts of fillings they can hide. You just need to make sure the fillings are not too wet. Be experimental – go for a black forest gateaux filling if you have a bit of cake leftover or throw some cherries and chocolate sponge in there. There are five options here but the possibilities are endless.

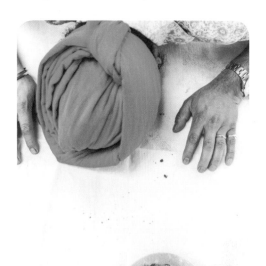

Serves 4–6 (makes about 24 samosas)

Samosas
500g plain flour
50g cocoa powder
1 tsp salt
1 tsp ajwain seeds or cumin seeds, toasted until fragrant
125ml rapeseed oil
warm water, to bind
vegetable oil, for deep-frying
whipped double cream, to serve (optional)

1 To make the samosas, sift the flour, cocoa powder and salt into a bowl. Add the toasted seeds then slowly add the oil and warm water until the mixture forms a workable dough. Shape it into a ball, wrap in cling film and rest it in the fridge for 1 hour.

2 Meanwhile prepare your chosen filling(s) (see overleaf).

3 Form the samosa dough into balls a wee bit bigger than a golf ball and roll each out into a circle about 15cm in diameter and 3mm thick. Cut each into two semi-circles and place on a baking sheet(s).

4 Add half a tablespoon of the filling to the middle of each semi-circle of dough and fold into a triangle. Repeat to use up all the filling.

5 Put a deep-fat fryer on to 170°C or fill a deep pan half full with vegetable oil and heat until a breadcrumb dropped in sizzles and turns golden brown in 30 seconds. Fry the samosas in small batches for 4–5 minutes, or until they have turned a deeper brown and are crisp. Remove from the oil with a slotted spoon and drain on kitchen paper. Serve alone or with whipped cream, as you prefer.

White chocolate ganache

200g white chocolate
100ml double cream
90ml milk
½ tsp salt

Break the chocolate into small pieces and put into a bowl. Bring the cream and milk to the boil, immediately remove from the heat and pour over the chocolate. Add the salt and then stir until the chocolate has melted completely. Chill until firm.

Raspberry compote

80g caster sugar
zest and juice of 1 lemon
300g raspberries
1 tbsp cornflour mixed with
3 tbsp cold water

Place the sugar and lemon juice in a pan and bring to the boil. Set aside a handful of the raspberries, then add the remainder to the pan. Leave the raspberries to soften slightly then strain the juice into a separate pan. Bubble the juice over a medium–high heat until reduced to a thick syrup, then add the cornflour and cook for a few minutes. Return the berries to the syrup, add the reserved whole raspberries and chill.

Lime and ginger curd

4 limes
juice of ½ orange
2 tsp corn flour
125g caster sugar
½ tsp ground ginger
20g fresh ginger, peeled and grated
4 eggs

Zest one lime and squeeze the juice from all four. Combine all the ingredients in a heatproof bowl, place over a simmering pan of water, making sure the bottom of the bowl doesn't touch the water, and cook until very thick – about 20–30 minutes. Chill until ready to use.

Spiced pear and raisin compote

400g pears, peeled, cored and cut into small dice
50g soft light brown sugar
2 tsp allspice
90g raisins

Place the pears in a pan with the sugar and allspice and heat until softened. Fold in the raisins then set aside to chill.

Pecan and maple syrup

130ml maple syrup
400g pecans

Finely grind 100g of the pecans in
a food processor and roughly chop
the remainder. In a pan, bring the
maple syrup to the boil. Add the
chopped pecans and mix well, then
stir in the ground nuts to bind well.
Set aside and chill.

Peach and maple-syrup pastries with lime crème fraîche

These pastries can be made a little ahead of time and kept in the fridge. They're great for picnics as well as afternoon teas and you can use any fruit that's in season – in the autumn I'd swap the peaches for plums.

Serves 6

500g ripe peaches
150ml maple syrup
1 x 250g packet good-quality filo
    pastry sheets
100g unsalted butter, melted
150g caster sugar
1 egg, beaten
zest and juice of 2 limes
200g crème fraîche or Greek yoghurt,
    to serve

1   Preheat the oven to 180°C/gas 4. Line a baking tray with greaseproof paper.

2   Stone the peaches, cut into quarters and then in half again. Place on a baking tray, drizzle with 100ml of the maple syrup and roast in the oven for about 7–8 minutes, until softened and slightly caramelised. Set aside to cool.

3   Lay out a sheet of the filo pastry on a clean work surface. Brush with melted butter and sprinkle with sugar. Repeat this with two more layers, so the pastry is three layers thick. Cut the pastry into 10cm squares.

4   Spoon some of the peach mixture on to the middle of the pastry. Brush the edges with the beaten egg and fold the pastry over corner to corner so you have a triangular-shaped pastry. Repeat with the remaining mix.

5   Brush the tops of the pastry triangles with more melted butter and the remaining maple syrup. Place on the prepared baking tray and bake in the oven for 12–15 minutes, or until light golden in colour.

6   Mix the lime zest and juice with the crème fraîche or yoghurt and serve alongside the pastries.

Triple chocolate brownies with jammy custard

Brownies are just so simple to make and never fail to please. They're also a great standby pud. Once baked, you can freeze any brownies you don't need and simply take them out and bake them when you're stuck for a last-minute dessert. Whip up the jammy custard or just serve with vanilla ice cream or whipped cream.

Makes 12

300g dark chocolate (60–70 per cent
  cocoa solids)
225g unsalted butter
3 eggs
225g sugar
225g self-raising flour
200g milk chocolate chips
200g white chocolate chips
1 x 450g jar good-quality jam
500ml shop-bought fresh custard

1 Preheat the oven to 160°C/gas 3. Line a deep baking tray with greaseproof paper.

2 Melt the dark chocolate and butter in a glass or metal bowl set over a pan of simmering water.

3 Meanwhile whisk the eggs with the sugar in a large bowl until pale and fluffy. Once thoroughly melted, fold the chocolate and butter mixture into the egg mixture. Combine well.

4 Sift the flour and fold this in also. Finally, fold in the milk and white chocolate chips. Spoon the mixture into the prepared baking tray and level the surface by tapping the tray on the work surface. Bake in the oven for 20 minutes, until the mixture has risen slightly and a crust has formed – they'll still be squidgy in the middle, just how I like them. Allow to cool completely before trimming off the crusts around the outside (if they emerge from the cutting without having been nibbled, these crusts are great folded into vanilla ice cream). Cut the bake into 12 squares.

5 For the jammy custard, heat as much jam as desired with a little water to slacken, then stir it through some thick pouring custard to get a lovely rippled effect. Serve hot or cold with the brownies.

Gypsy tart

This is a very, very sweet tart from the Isle of Sheppey in Kent, not known to many outside the region, which is a great shame, especially for pud-lovers like me. The coconut ice cream I serve with it gives my sweet tooth the extra sugar fix it needs but you could also serve it with crème fraîche or Greek yoghurt to cut through its richness.

Serves 8

Pastry
75g caster sugar
150g butter
1 egg, beaten
225g plain flour, plus extra for dusting
  the work surface

Filling
375g condensed milk
225g evaporated milk
225g muscovado sugar (dark or light)

To serve
coconut ice cream

1 Make the pastry by creaming the sugar and butter together in a bowl. Add the beaten egg, and when well mixed in, add the flour. Form into a dough, wrap in cling film and leave to rest in the fridge for 1 hour.

2 Preheat the oven to 180°C/gas 4. Roll out the pastry on a lightly floured surface and use to line a 25cm tart case, letting the pastry hang over the edges of the tin to allow for shrinkage. Prick with a fork, line with greaseproof paper and baking beans and bake in the oven for 10 minutes. Remove the greaseproof paper and baking beans and return the tart case to the oven for a further 5 minutes to dry out the base. Remove, then reduce the oven temperature to 160°C/gas 3.

3 To make the tart filling, combine the condensed and evaporated milk with the muscovado sugar and whisk until light and fluffy. Place the filling in the partly baked case and cook for about 20–25 minutes until just set. Remove from the oven and allow to cool.

4 Serve warm or at room temperature with a scoop of coconut ice cream.

White chocolate and crushed nut muffins with herbed honey

For me, these are breakfast muffins: chocolate at breakfast might be pure decadence but there's only a hint here, and the honey mixed with mint and basil adds fresh but also floral notes.

Makes 12 muffins

125g mixed nuts (any you like)
300g self-raising flour
125g caster sugar
2 eggs, beaten
150ml buttermilk
75ml sunflower oil
30g white chocolate chips
125g set honey
1 tbsp finely sliced mint
1 tbsp finely sliced basil

1 Preheat the oven to 180°C/gas 4.

2 Spread out the mixed nuts on a baking tray and toast in the oven for 10 minutes. Roughly chop and set aside to cool.

3 Sift the flour and sugar together in a large bowl. Make a well in the centre.

4 In a separate bowl, mix the eggs, buttermilk and oil. Add the egg mixture to the flour and sugar and quickly bring together using a balloon whisk – do not over-mix or the muffins will be tough. Very gently fold in the chopped nuts.

5 Divide the mixture between 12 muffin cases – about 2 tablespoons of mixture per case – then push 4–5 white chocolate chips into the centre of each.

6 Bake in the oven for 30 minutes, then allow to cool slightly.

7 Meanwhile, gently warm the honey in a small pan and mix in the mint and basil. Drizzle some herbed honey on top of each muffin before serving.

Gingerbread pudding with jammy figs

You could also use Madeira cake or any other cake for this pud. Fresh is great, but if it's a little bit stale that's fine too as it will soak up the custard and jammy figs.

Serves 6–8

500ml double cream
300ml milk
2 tsp ground ginger
8 eggs, plus 2 egg yolks
100g caster sugar
1 good-quality shop-bought
  gingerbread loaf
2 tbsp melted butter
  or 1 tbsp icing sugar
40g raspberry jam
10 black figs, stalks removed,
  or tinned figs

1 Preheat the oven to 150°C/gas 2. Line a deep baking tray or loaf tin with greaseproof paper.

2 In a pan, bring the cream, milk and ginger to a simmer.

3 Whisk the eggs, yolks and sugar together in a bowl then pour the hot liquid over them. Whisk well.

4 Cut the gingerbread loaf into 3cm dice. Place in the prepared tray or tin and pour over the egg custard to cover. Leave to stand for about 20 minutes to soak.

5 Bake in the oven for about 30 minutes, or until a skewer comes out clean. Brush the top of the pudding with the melted butter, or dust with the icing sugar.

6 For the jammy figs, warm the jam in a pan, adding a tablespoon of water to loosen if desired. Cut the figs in half and add to the melted jam. Spoon on to a baking tray and place in the oven for about 10 minutes, or until the figs are nice and sticky and caramelised.

7 Serve the jammy figs with the warm pudding.

Voodoo doughnuts

These baked doughnuts are healthier than their sinful deep-fried cousins but they will still put you under their spell. That little bit of chilli spice in the chocolate custard filling is magical.

Makes about 24

30g caster sugar
13g fast-action dried yeast
225ml milk, warmed to body
    temperature, plus extra cold milk
    for brushing
570g strong white bread flour, plus
    extra for dusting the work surface
1 tsp salt
6 medium eggs
100g softened unsalted butter, cut into
    small pieces
granulated sugar, to dust

Chocolate chilli custard filling

500ml milk
¼ tsp dried chilli flakes
150g dark chocolate
    (minimum 60 per cent cocoa solids),
    broken into small pieces
6 medium eggs
75g caster sugar
35g plain flour
25g cocoa powder

To save time...
I just snip a tiny bit of the end off a plastic food bag to use as a piping bag but you could use a piping bag with a very fine nozzle.

1 Start with the filling. Put the milk, chilli flakes and chocolate in a pan over a medium heat and bring to the boil. Stir now and again so that the chocolate doesn't stick to the bottom of the pan and burn.

2 Meanwhile, mix the eggs, sugar, flour and cocoa powder in a large bowl and beat well with a whisk until there are no lumps.

3 Pour the boiling chocolate milk over the cocoa mixture and whisk well then pour back into the pan and bring to the boil over a medium heat. Cook for 5 minutes, stirring constantly. Pour into a bowl through a sieve to catch any lumps, then cover the top with cling film to stop any skin forming. Let it cool before filling the doughnuts.

4 For the doughnuts, dissolve the sugar and the yeast in the warm milk. Sift the flour and salt into the bowl of an electric mixer fitted with a dough hook, then gradually pour in the milk, mixing on a medium speed. When fully mixed, add the eggs one at a time. Lastly, add the soft butter in three stages and mix well.

5 Knead the mixture to a smooth dough using the machine then cover with a piece of oiled cling film and let it stand in the bowl until it has doubled in size.

6 Knead it again to remove the air (knock back the dough). Roll out to 2–3cm thick on a lightly floured surface then cut out rounds from the dough using a 7cm cutter. Place these doughnuts on a baking tray lined with greaseproof paper. Cover lightly with oiled cling film and leave them to rise again.

7 Preheat the oven to 180°C/gas 4. Bake the doughnuts in the oven for 15–20 minutes until fully risen and golden in colour.

7 Fill the doughnuts as soon as they come out the oven. Pierce a hole in the doughnuts and, using a piping bag, pipe in the chocolate filling.

8 Gently brush the doughnuts with milk then dust with sugar. (The sugar can be mixed with a little chilli powder for a bit of heat!) Serve immediately – hopefully still a little warm.

Turkish coffee and cardamom mousse

Chocolate mousse, but given a distinctly Eastern spin. Cardamom, rose and
pistachio whack it with fragrance and crunch and make this a lovely grown-up pud.

Serves 6–8

500g white chocolate,
   broken into pieces
4 tbsp instant coffee granules
20g green cardamoms, lightly bashed
400g whipping cream
2 gelatine leaves
3 egg whites
100g icing sugar
30g pistachios, toasted and crushed
rose water, to taste

1 Melt the white chocolate in a bowl set over simmering water,
making sure the base of the bowl doesn't touch the water, then set
aside and leave to cool to body temperature.

2 Boil 250ml water in a pan, add the coffee and stir to combine, then
add the bruised cardamoms and simmer until you are left with 150ml
of liquid. Remove the pods and leave to cool to body temperature.

3 Whip 250g of the cream until when you lift the whisk it leaves a
ribbon trail (semi-whipped).

4 Soak the gelatine leaves in cold water until softened. Squeeze out
the excess water and add the leaves to the warm coffee. Mix well
then pour into the semi-whipped cream and combine thoroughly. Fold
this mixture into the melted white chocolate. The mixture might become a
little grainy at this stage; if so, just whisk it until smooth. Add the pistachios,
reserving a few to sprinkle on top at the end.

5 Place the egg whites in a spotlessly clean bowl, then, by hand
or using an electric hand whisk, whisk the whites until they stand up
in stiff peaks when the whisk is lifted. Now ramp up the speed and start
to add the sugar, a tablespoon at a time. Beat for 3 or 4 seconds between
each addition and continue until all the sugar has been added. When ready,
the mixture should be thick and glossy. Fold this meringue mix into the
chocolate mixture.

6 Spoon or pipe this chocolate mousse into glasses, bowls or moulds
and allow to set in the fridge for at least 2 hours.

7 Whip the remaining cream and add rose water to taste. Spoon this
on top of the mousses and sprinkle with the reserved pistachios.

Biscotti and crowdie dip

If you've never had crowdie before you are in for a treat, and it is well worth trying to track down this fresh Scottish cheese as it is quite unique. The flavour is similar to cottage cheese – slightly sour – but it has a smoother, soft, crumbly texture, and it's a great carrier for other flavours. It's often served with oatcakes, but by sweetening it with a little honey and balancing out the acidity with some lemon juice, these sweet biscotti make the perfect accompaniment for dipping.

Serves 12

Biscotti
300g caster sugar
300g plain flour
15g baking powder
5 eggs, beaten
150g mixed peel
150g mixed nuts

Crowdie dip
150g crowdie cheese or cream cheese
2 tbsp clear honey
zest and juice of 1 lemon

1 Preheat the oven to 170°C/Gas 3½ and line a shallow 40 x 30cm baking tray with greaseproof paper.

2 To make the biscotti, sift the sugar, flour and baking powder together. Add the beaten eggs to the mixture and beat with a wooden spoon until you have a batter consistency. Stir in the mixed peel and nuts then spoon the mixture into the prepared tray, flattening it down well.

3 Bake for about 40 minutes until risen and golden. Remove from the oven and chill. Once chilled, slice lengthways into very thin slices and place these back on a baking tray in the oven for about 20 minutes, until toasted and crunchy.

4 To make the crowdie dip, mix the cheese with the honey and stir in the lemon zest and juice. Serve the biscotti slightly warm if desired.

Sticky toffee skewers with cashew-nut custard

Make a sticky toffee pudding as normal but cut it up and pop it on a skewer basted with caramel sauce and nuts – just a different way to have your cake and eat it!

Serves 8

350g pitted dates
600ml water
100g softened unsalted butter
350g soft dark brown sugar
4 eggs
350g self-raising flour
2 tsp bicarbonate of soda

Sticky toffee sauce

270g caster sugar
600ml double cream

Cashew-nut custard

100g cashew nuts
200ml milk
600g pouring custard

1　Preheat the oven to 150°C/gas 2. Fill a roasting tin with hot water and put in the oven to make steam – this will make the sponge moist and help it to rise well. Line a 22cm-square tin with greaseproof paper.

2　Put the dates and water in a saucepan and bring to the boil. Simmer until soft, then blend to a purée and set aside.

3　Cream the butter and sugar. Add the eggs, then gradually then sift in the flour and bicarbonate of soda and fold in. Add the date purée and fold in.

4　Pour the mixture into the prepared tin and bake in the oven for 1–1½ hours. To check it's ready, insert a skewer into the middle of the cake – if it comes out clean it's ready; if it has wet mix on it bake for a further 5 minutes and check again.

5　Once cooked, leave the cake to cool, then wrap it in cling film and chill. When it is cold, cut it into small cubes and thread these on to eight thin skewers.

6　To make the sticky toffee sauce, cook the sugar slowly in a large pan (be warned: it will expand to six times the volume of the cream when you add it). When it is a dark golden colour, take off the heat, and then very carefully and gradually add the cream. Take care as it will bubble up. Stir well, put the pan back on the heat and when it comes to the boil again, take off the heat and put to one side.

7　For the cashew-nut custard, heat the grill to high. Place the cashews in a baking tray and grill, turning them constantly until they are a nice golden brown. Remove and leave to cool for a few minutes then roughly chop them.

8　Bring the milk to the boil and add the cashews. Simmer for 2 minutes, then stir in the custard.

9　To serve, brush the cake skewers with the sticky toffee sauce and serve the cashew-nut custard and extra toffee sauce on the side.

Egg and soldiers

This is what I used to make for the kids when they were younger, as they had egg cups that fit really neatly into a tray so that we could poach them in the oven. Basically it's a crème brûlée mix and the 'soldiers' are lovely biscotti. Feel free to try different flavours in your custard or in the soldiers.

Serves 6

Egg custard
10 egg yolks
500ml cream
100g caster sugar
1 vanilla pod, split and deseeded

Soldiers
250g caster sugar
250g flour
1½ baking powder
4 eggs
30g sultanas
30g raisins
120g hazelnuts, toasted and crushed

1. Preheat the oven to 160°C/gas 3. Line a 40 x 30cm shallow baking tray with greaseproof paper.

2. To make the soldiers, sift the sugar, flour and baking powder together in a bowl.

3. Beat the egg, then add to the bowl. Mix until you have a thick batter, then add the dried fruit and hazelnuts. Pour the batter into the prepared tray and bake in the oven for about 35–45 minutes, until risen and lightly golden on top.

4. Remove the biscuits from the oven and chill. Once cool, cut in half lengthways, then slice along the length to make soldiers that are 20cm long by 5mm wide. Return them to the oven for 20 minutes, until they are toasted and crunchy, then remove.

5. Turn the oven down to 130°C/gas ¾ for the egg custards.

6. Place the egg yolks in a large bowl. In a pan, bring the cream, sugar and vanilla to a simmer, then remove from the heat and pour over the egg yolks, whisking rapidly until well mixed and thickened. Pour the mixture through a sieve to remove any egg albumen, and skim off any froth with a small ladle.

7. Pour the mixture into shallow ovenproof bowls, ramekins or egg cups. Place these in a deep oven tray and fill halfway up the sides with water.

8. Bake in the oven for about 35 minutes until the custards are very nearly set but still have a slight wobble in the middle. Take the tray out and allow the residual heat to finish the cooking process so as to avoid overcooking the custards. Allow to cool, then serve with the soldiers.

Nutella pancake gateau

This is a dish that came about thanks to a drink-fuelled party and a challenge: 'You're a chef, rustle us up something sweet to eat'. Thus the Nutella gateau was born. You generally always have flour, eggs and milk in the house to make pancakes. Fill them with Nutella and bake in the oven. Simple as that.

Serves 12

1 x 750g jar Nutella hazelnut spread
50g hazelnuts, toasted and crushed

Pancakes
250g plain flour
50g caster sugar
4 eggs
500ml milk
75g melted butter
vegetable oil, for frying

Marmalade sauce
1 x 450g jar of quality marmalade
   (any type – with peel or without)
100g butter
250ml orange juice
100ml Cointreau

1 To make the pancake batter, sift the flour and sugar into a bowl. Whisk in the eggs, then slowly add the milk to this mixture, whisking it in. Finally, whisk in the melted butter and strain through a sieve to remove any small lumps.

2 Heat a thin film of oil in a large frying pan over a medium heat and fry the pancakes one by one, cooking to a light golden on each side before removing to a cooling rack.

3 Preheat the oven to 160°C/gas 3½.

4 Once the pancakes are completely cool, warm the Nutella. You can either place the jar in a pan of just-boiled water (off the heat) for 10 minutes or transfer it to a bowl and microwave for 30 seconds on high, until soft. Spread each pancake with a thin layer of warm Nutella (you need to spread them before you start to layer as it's difficult to spread them once they're stacked). Place one pancake, Nutella-side up, in a large ovenproof dish with sides or in the frying pan in which you cooked the pancakes (provided it's ovenproof). Place another pancake on top, then keep building your gateau until you run out of pancakes.

5 To make the marmalade sauce, heat the marmalade with the butter, orange juice and Cointreau. Bring to the boil and simmer for 2 minutes or until syrupy.

6 Pour half the sauce over the gateau and bake in the oven for 30 minutes. Check it's ready by inserting a metal skewer into the centre, count to five, then take it out – it should be piping hot. Towards the end of the cooking time, warm through some of the reserved sauce and serve with the gateau.

06 PANDORA'S BOX

This chapter contains the things you need when you want to make something tasty in a hurry – when the munchies grab you, when you're back from work late, when you need to impress that foodie who has brought the latest, handpicked, hand-dried, hand-cut, hand-painted salt from the far reaches of the Himalayas… It's the box of tricks that will give you flavour, flavour, flavour. You'll find spice rubs, sauces, dressings, marinades, some useful bulkier accompaniments, such as perfect steamed rice, and my Scottish essential – the tattie scone, as well as plenty of chutneys.

'Chutney' is a word that describes a family of condiments from Asia but is often misunderstood. It conjures up jars of exotic flavours and spices that take hours of slow cooking or the skill of an alchemist to enable the fruit and veg to be pickled and preserved for months. And don't even get me started on the dodgy luminous stuff served at some Asian restaurants… The Indian word refers to fresh and pickled preparations indiscriminately, with the preserves often being sweetened, but several Indian languages use the word for fresh preparations only, as we do in our house. A different word – 'achar' – applies to preserves and pickles that are made using acidic liquids, citric juices, tamarind or the magic of fermentation. To go into that would require a whole book so I will be looking solely at chutneys in the way we make them at home – their fresh, zesty incarnations. I am going to show you that with a bit of TLC, making chutney is something that can be mastered easily. Fresh chutneys may be wet or dry, have a coarse or a fine texture and they can be whipped up in moments. They are always, always, packed full of punchy flavours.

Tattie scone

The name is somewhat deceptive as this is nothing like the fluffy afternoon scone served with clotted cream and jam. A tattie scone is more like a griddled flatbread, traditionally made with leftover potatoes fried in loads of butter. In my opinion, it is a stroke of Scottish genius – comforting, hearty and robust enough to keep out the somewhat inclement weather we are known to suffer up here. Tattie scones also have special significance for me, as they were one of the first things I leaned to make as a young chef on the breakfast shift at the Mount Royal Hotel in Edinburgh.

Serves 4

500g floury potatoes, baked in their skins
50g unsalted butter
125g plain flour, plus extra to dust
salt and pepper
freshly grated nutmeg, to taste

1 Preheat the oven to 200°C/gas 6.

2 Prick the potatoes all over, place on a baking tray and bake for about 45 minutes, until really soft in the middle.

3 Once the tatties come out of the oven and are cool enough to handle, cut them in half and scoop the flesh out of the skins. Add the butter and mash, then stir in the flour. Season with salt, pepper and nutmeg, to taste.

4 Roll out the dough on a lightly floured work surface to about 5mm, then cut around a 15cm side plate to shape.

5 Dust lightly with flour and prick the scone well. You can either freeze the mixture at this point or cook according to the recipe (see pages 24 and 110).

Steamed rice

For perfect steamed rice you will need a heavy-based pan with a tight-fitting lid so that the precious steam does not escape.

Serves 4–6

basmati rice, measured up to the 400ml mark on a measuring jug
600ml water
1 tbsp toasted sesame seed oil
100g black and white sesame seeds
dark soy sauce, to taste

1 Wash the rice in cold water until the water runs clear.

2 Pop the rice in the pan with the water – you should have about 2.5cm of water above the rice (a knuckle segment of your finger is how I measure it). Bring to the boil.

3 Boil until most of the surface liquid has evaporated – about 10–15 minutes – and the surface of the rice has small potholes on it.

4 Now cover the pot with a very tight-fitting lid, turn the heat down as low as possible and let the rice cook undisturbed for 15 minutes.

5 Take the pan off the heat and let it rest for 5 minutes. Meanwhile, grease the insides of four ramekins or dariole moulds with the sesame oil, then coat with the sesame seeds (keep any leftover seeds for another recipe).

6 Pack the moulds with the rice, pour a splash of soy into each and turn out on to plates to serve.

Soda bread

Freshly made bread gives a unique type of hug: a warm, comforting aroma that fills the house with the promise of good stuff to come. Yet so many of us don't have the time every day for the kneading and proving that regular bread-making requires. Enter soda bread – TLC in a loaf, with all the joy of the fresh bake, yet without any of the faff.

Serves 4

140g plain flour, plus extra for dusting
140g self-raising wholemeal flour
1 tsp baking powder
1 tsp fine sea salt
125ml cold water
125ml buttermilk or thin yoghurt

1 Preheat the oven to 200°C/gas 6. Lightly dust a baking sheet with flour. Tip the plain and self-raising flour, baking powder and salt into a large mixing bowl and stir.

2 Make a well in the centre of the mixture, and gradually stir in the cold water and buttermilk, until combined. The mixture will be quite wet so leave it to stand for 5 minutes.

3 Shape the dough into a round on the baking sheet. Leave to stand for 10 minutes before baking.

5 Cut a 4cm cross (1cm deep) on the top of the dough with a floured knife. Bake in the oven for about 30 minutes or until the loaf sounds hollow when tapped. Cool on a wire rack.

Pickled cucumber and tomatoes

This is one for the summer, when tomatoes are really flavoursome. It can make a simple salad sing or you can use it to add a home-made element to a picnic spread of smoked fish and cold meats.

Fills a 1-litre jar

250ml white wine vinegar
250ml water
200g caster sugar
25g tarragon
25g thyme sprigs
10 bay leaves
good pinch of saffron threads
2 garlic bulbs, split into cloves (no need to peel)
250g plum tomatoes, halved lengthways, deseeded and cut into petals
1 cucumber, peeled and sliced

1. Place all the ingredients except the tomatoes and cucumbers into a pan. Bring to the boil and simmer for 5 minutes, then remove from the heat. Let the liquid cool to just above body temperature then quickly place the tomatoes and cucumbers in sterilised jars (see page 241). Strain the pickling liquid and pour over.

2. Seal the jars and leave for 1–2 days, if you can, but for at least 6 hours before using. The pickle will just keep getting more and more flavour in the fridge and will last about 2 weeks.

Dill pickle and onions

You can use this pickle right away but it gets better after an hour and keeps getting better the longer you leave it in the fridge. Serve it with burgers or hot roast meat sandwiches. It's cracking with a ploughman's lunch or nice just added to a bit of good rapeseed oil to give a salad dressing texture.

Makes enough to serve 12 or more

250g sliced dill pickle from a jar
250g red onions, finely sliced
juice of 2 limes
2 tbsp vinegar from the dill pickle jar
1 tsp chopped thyme
½ tsp dried chilli flakes
1 tbsp caster sugar
large pinch of salt

1. Put all of the ingredients in a bowl and mix well. Pop in a jar and store in the fridge – it will keep for up to 3 weeks.

Peach and chilli relish

One for the summer – ripe peaches are essential. You can swap the peaches for other stone fruits, if you like.

Makes enough to serve 4–6

3 ripe peaches
1 tbsp chopped preserved ginger
2 tbsp brown sugar
2 tbsp sherry vinegar
2 tsp soy sauce
1 red Thai chilli, chopped (seeds and all)
salt and pepper, to taste

1 Put the peaches in a large bowl, pour over boiling water to cover them and leave for 1 minute, then fish them out and put them into cold water for 2 minutes.

2 Peel the peaches, cut in half and discard the stone, then chop the peach into 1cm cubes (if they have a wee bit of skin left on them that's okay) and place in a bowl.

3 In a pan, bring the rest of the ingredients to the boil and pour over the peaches. Cover the bowl with cling film and leave for 30 minutes, then taste and add more seasoning if necessary. The relish will keep for a few days in the fridge.

Sweet red pepper and coconut chutney

This is a hot South Indian chutney. If you're not a fan of chilli, you can reduce the number just to one or two chillies, or even leave them out completely.

Makes enough to serve 4

1 coconut, peeled and chopped
3 tbsp white wine vinegar
5 dried red chillies
½ tsp asafoetida
3 tbsp vegetable oil
3 tsp black peppercorns
1 tsp mustard seeds
½ red pepper, cored, deseeded and finely diced
salt

1 Put the coconut pieces into the bowl of a food processor. Whizz to get a finely grated coconut mixture. Add the vinegar and whizz to combine.

2 Toast the chillies in a dry pan over a medium heat, then break into small pieces and set them aside.

3 Heat a heavy-based pan over a high heat and add the oil. When the oil is hot, add the black peppercorns and fry until aromatic, then add the mustard seeds and fry till they start to pop, then immediately take the pan off the heat. Add the red chillies and asafoetida and leave until the chillies stop sizzling.

4 Scrape the coconut mixture into to a bowl and add the red pepper and spiced oil. Mix well and season with salt to taste.

Mint and coriander chutney

This is my mum's recipe and we always have it in the house. It's as important as having salt and pepper on the table.

Makes enough to serve 6–8

200g coriander leaves
150g mint leaves
5 garlic cloves
2.5cm piece of fresh ginger
2 green chillies
1 tbsp caster sugar
3 tsp distilled white vinegar
salt

1 Whizz all the ingredients into a smooth paste in a food processor or blender.

2 Season with salt to taste. Chill and serve.

Variation
To make this into a mint and coriander sauce, mix to taste with up to 300g Greek yoghurt.

Chunky piccalili

Piccalilli, the mustardy veg-packed pickle, is a proper British classic and such a winner. This is a traditional recipe from my friend Mr Pott's mum. I make it in big batches in late summer or the start of autumn so that it's ready for winter, just when you need that spicy lift to your lunch. I just love the sharp, nose-tingling punchiness of it and have it with cold meats, cheeses and bangers and mash.

Makes 2 litres

1 small cauliflower, broken into small pieces
2 celery sticks, roughly chopped
2 courgettes, roughly chopped
2 red peppers, roughly chopped
1 carrot, roughly chopped
1½ tbsp sea salt
2 tbsp plain flour
450ml cider vinegar
100g caster sugar
2 tbsp yellow mustard seeds
1 tbsp ground turmeric
1 tbsp mustard powder
2 tsp chilli powder
seeds from 20 green cardamom pods

1   Place the vegetables in a large bowl, sprinkle with the salt, cover with cling film and leave to stand overnight. The next day, rinse the vegetables and drain.

3   Blend the flour with 100ml of the vinegar and set aside. Pour the remaining the vinegar into a large saucepan and add the sugar, mustard seeds, turmeric, mustard powder, chilli powder and cardamom seeds. Bring slowly to the boil and simmer for 5 minutes, stirring until the sugar has dissolved.

4   Add the vegetables to the pan, bring back to the boil and simmer for 5 minutes. Add the flour mixture to the pan, bring back to the boil and simmer for a further 5 minutes or until the mixture is thick.

5   Remove from the heat. Pack the vegetables and pickling liquid into warm, sterilised jars (see page 241). When cool, label and date. Store in a cool, dark place for at least 2 weeks before opening to allow the flavours to mellow.

Chippy sauce

If you're Scottish, this needs no introduction – it's the essential accompaniment to a fish supper. For more about it, see page 90.

Makes about 600g

1 x 320g bottle of Gold Star sauce (or 425g bottle of HP sauce if unavailable)
140ml malt vinegar
1½ tbsp caster sugar

1. Mix all the ingredients together and check the seasoning. The sauce will keep in a sterilised bottle (see below) in the fridge for up to 1 month.

Chippy sauce with a kick
Follow the instructions above but increase the sugar to 3 tablespoons and add 1 level teaspoon chilli powder.

Note
The easiest way to sterilise bottles or jars is to run them through a hot programme in a dishwasher. Alternatively, you can wash them in warm, soapy water then leave them to dry in an oven set at 140°C/gas 1.

Easy squeezy cheese sauce

I do love those 'plastic' cheese slices, so this is my way of making that guilty pleasure a bit more proper! This squeezy cheese sauce is almost like a fondue and will convert your desire for the cheap and nasty into one for the slick and tasty. Serve with burgers, hot dogs, nachos or whatever else you like. Squeezy bottle optional.

Makes enough to serve 6–8

150g Gruyère cheese
150g Emmental cheese
100g Red Leicester
200ml white wine
4 tsp cornflour
½ tsp garlic purée
salt and pepper

1   Grate all the cheeses into a large bowl.

2   Stir the cornflour into the white wine until it is dissolved. Pour this mixture into a heavy-based pan, add the garlic purée and bring just to the boil, stirring all the time with a whisk. Add the grated cheese and stir until melted and bubbling. Season with salt and pepper and stir well.

3   You can now either serve the sauce right from the pan or pour it into a squeezy bottle (I keep used ketchup bottles), in which case, pop the bottle in a pan of simmering water over a low heat to keep the sauce liquid.

4   Once cool, it will keep in the fridge for a week or two, but remember to store it in a suitable container as you will need to cut it up once it is cold to melt it down again before using.

Variations
You can spice up this sauce by adding chopped green serrano chillies to the mix, but you'll need to cut the hole in the squeezy bottle wider so the bits can come out. Or you can use up all your leftover bits of cheese – there's so much cheesy fun to be had.

Tamarind and date sauce

Tamarind and date chutney is an essential condiment throughout the Punjab, and enjoying some of the region's lip-smacking street foods without the chutney alongside is unimaginable. Having a supply of this Punjab-inspired sauce in your fridge takes care off all kinds of cravings. Pop it on a burger or a grilled sausage, or let it down with a bit of water and pour it over oysters. It's a go-to staple for my kids to jazz up their food or just as a dip for Pringles, nachos or vegetable sticks. This quantity would be enough for 16–20 folk if you were dishing it out at once but it's a good amount to have stocked in the fridge – though, once tasted, it's likely to disappear quickly!

Makes about 400ml

2 tamarind blocks, covered with cold water and allowed to soak overnight
200g pitted dates
50g fennel seeds
25g chilli flakes
25g black peppercorns
20g ground cumin
10 star anise
2 whole cloves
3 litres water
about 150g sugar, to taste
salt, to taste

1 Place all the ingredients except the sugar and salt in a pan. Bring to the boil and simmer for 2 hours. Stir often and watch out as the mixture will start to spit.

2 Once it has thickened nicely, add sugar and salt to taste – it should have a sweet and sour tang with all the spice and heat in the background – then leave to cool slightly. Pass through a sieve while it is still warm rather than cold as it will thicken as it cools.

3 Keep in the fridge for up to 1 month in an airtight container.

Tomato salsa

I could never understand why when my mates had a barbecue they bought the best meat for their burgers and local, hand-made, top-quality sausages and then served them with a mass-produced tasteless tomato relish… So I made them this salsa. Boys, here's the recipe – use it!

Makes enough to serve 6

300g ripe plum tomatoes, halved, deseeded and
   chopped into 5mm dice
3 shallots or ½ small red onion, finely chopped
1 bunch spring onions, finely chopped
150g tomato ketchup
150g Thai sweet chilli sauce (the Healthy Boy brand
   if you can get it)
juice of 1 lemon
juice of 1 lime
3 tbsp chopped coriander
salt and pepper

1 Place all the ingredients in a bowl and mix well. Check the seasoning then leave to rest until using. It will keep for up to 2 weeks stored in the fridge.

Sweet mango and lime sauce

A great sweet and sour sauce – useful as a dip, on burgers and with grilled meat and fish

Makes enough to serve 10–12

1 x 350g jar sweet mango chutney
juice of 8 limes
4 tbsp water

1 Blend all the ingredients using a hand blender and pass through a sieve.

2 Store in a sterilised container (see page 241) in the fridge for up to 1 month.

Ras el hanout

Although this Moroccan spice mix can contain anything up to 100 spices, mine is not that mental. If you get stuck there are some good shop-bought mixes available.

Serves 6

4 tsp ground ginger
4 tsp ground cardamon
4 tsp ground mace
3 tsp sumac
2 tsp ground cinnamon
2 tsp ground allspice
2 tsp ground coriander seeds
2 tsp ground nutmeg
2 tsp turmeric
1 tsp ground black pepper
1 tsp ground white pepper
1 tsp ground cayenne pepper
1 tsp ground anise seeds
1 tsp ground cumin
1 tsp smoked sweet paprika
1 tsp dried thyme
pinch ground cloves

1   Mix all of the spices well in a bowl. Transfer to an airtight container and store in a dry, dark place; it will keep for up to 3 months.

Chilli jam

The jam can be used straightaway, hot or cold, and will keep in the fridge for at least 1 week. It's great with grilled meat and fish, on top of steaks or used in sandwiches. I like it served in a baked potato with butter and grated Cheddar – grilled until the cheese melts and mixes with the sauce.

Makes enough to serve 6–8

50ml sesame oil
6 banana shallots, finely chopped
6 large red chillies, deseeded and finely chopped
3 garlic cloves, crushed to a purée
7.5cm piece fresh ginger, peeled and finely chopped
120g palm sugar or brown sugar
3 tbsp rice vinegar
3 tbsp hoisin sauce
35ml whisky
salt and pepper

1 Place the sesame oil in a heavy-bottomed pan and fry the shallots, chilli, garlic and ginger over a medium heat. When they begin to sizzle keep the heat moderate and cook for about 7 minutes. Add the palm sugar, turn up the heat and when it starts to caramelise add the vinegar and cook for 1 minute.

2 Take off the heat, add the hoisin and season, then stir in the whisky. It should be enough to add a rounded, slightly bitter finish to the sweet and hot taste of the jam. Season to taste.

3 Serve hot or cold, then store in the fridge for up to a week.

Red wine dressing

The wine makes it sound like this dressing is going to be heavy but reducing it keeps it sweet and syrupy – a bit like a balsamic vinegar. It can transform simple grilled, steamed or poached seafood.

Makes 350ml

150ml red wine
3 tbsp caster sugar
50ml sherry vinegar
salt and pepper
250ml vegetable oil
50ml rapeseed oil

1   Place the red wine and sugar in a pan over a high heat and bubble until reduced to a syrupy consistency (you should have 50ml).

2   Place the syrup in a bowl with the vinegar and add a pinch each of salt and pepper. Stir to dissolve.

3   Add the oils and whisk to an emulsion. Taste and adjust the seasoning if necessary.

Aioli

This fragrant tangy garlicky sauce from Provence is like summer sun in a jar. Its flavour is fresh and punchy and takes me back to a great summer holidaying in France. Wonderful as a condiment for all hot or cold seafood, meat and raw or cooked veg, it can also be used as a spread in a sandwich. I have even, in a moment of weakness, had it with chips and fried eggs!

Serves 6–8

10 garlic cloves, peeled
pinch of saffron threads
splash of Pernod
300g mayonnaise
salt and pepper

1 Mash the garlic cloves to a fine pulp with the saffron and Pernod. Beat this into the mayonnaise. Season to taste and serve. Any left over will keep in the fridge for up to a fortnight.

Spice mix

Unsurprisingly, I have countless spice mixes up my sleeve, but this particular mix was born to serve with the 'Kentucky deep-fried rabbit' I made when representing Scotland in a heat of the Great British Menu series. I was hooked and now serve it with anything I can. It's an essential with my Krispy Chicken Wings (see page 81), but I also sprinkle it over boiled veggies, grilled fish, even popcorn! The list is endless – it just adds that zing when you need it.

Makes enough to serve 10 or more

2 tbsp paprika
2 tbsp onion powder
2 tbsp garlic powder
2 tsp dried sage
2 tsp ground allspice
2 tsp chilli powder
2 tsp ground black pepper
2 tsp vegetable stock powder (I use Marigold bouillon powder)
1 tsp celery salt

1 Mix all of the spices in a bowl. Transfer to an airtight container and store in a dry, dark place. It will keep for up to 3 months.

Hazelnut dukkah

There are as many types of dukkah as there are people who make it and this is my version. Dukkah means 'to pound or crush' so it should be a dry crushed mixture not a paste. It's great as a sprinkle or as a dip and can be stored for several months in a sealed jar.

Makes enough to serve 6–8

4 tbsp sesame seeds
1½ tbsp coriander seeds
1 tbsp cumin seeds
½ tbsp fennel seeds
150g hazelnuts, peeled if possible,
   but don't worry too much about this
½ tsp chilli powder
½ tsp salt
¼ tsp pepper

1   Preheat the oven to 200°C/gas 6.

2   Put the seeds on one baking tray and the hazelnuts on another and roast in the oven for 5–10 minutes, or until they begin to colour and release an aroma. Remove, tip out of the trays and let them cool.

3   Pound the nuts and seeds in a mortar and pestle with the chilli powder, salt and pepper till roughly crushed, or put everything into a food processor and pulse till roughly ground.

Chilli sauce

A punchy, fast and easy chilli sauce, this is an essential for spice heads – I always have a batch of it in the fridge.

Makes enough for 8–10

100g coriander (stalks and leaves)
1 small white onion, chopped
6 garlic cloves, peeled and roughly chopped
6 green finger chillies, trimmed and chopped (the more seeds left in, the hotter the result)
cold water (same quantity as the lime juice)
1 tbsp caster sugar
½ tsp salt
juice of 2 limes

1   Blend the coriander, onion, garlic, green chilli and water using a hand blender. Add the sugar, salt and lime juice and mix well. This will keep in the fridge for up to 4 days if you can resist it that long! The colour will change but it will still be punchy.

Spiced pickled onions

These onions are a staple on the Singh table; I eat them with everything. I was given the recipe by Seghal, head chef at my former restaurant Roti, but I have tweaked it a bit and added the pomegranate molasses; they add that sweet but sour counterfoil to the sharpness of the vinegar and lime.

Serves 6–8

500g red onions, finely sliced
juice of 2 limes
2 tbsp distilled white vinegar (I use pickling vinegar)
1½ tbsp pomegranate molasses
chilli flakes, to taste

1. Put all the ingredients in a large bowl and mix well then pack into a sterilised 750ml–1-litre sealable jar (see page 241 to find out how best to sterilise your jar).

2. Leave for at least 3 hours, shaking it every now and then. It's best if kept for a week in the fridge before serving as the flavours will develop with time. If you store it, shake it from time to time. Once the jar has been opened, the onions will keep for up to a month in the fridge.

Soy and ginger sauce

This is a great sauce or dip for seafood – cooked or raw – or drizzled over a crisp radish salad. It can also be used with meat – grill a chicken breast that has been basted with the sauce – and then serve the rest on the side with some Steamed Rice (see page 234). Healthy and tasty.

Serves 6–8 as a dip

150ml dark soya sauce
4 tbsp finely diced carrot
3 tbsp finely diced sweet stem ginger
2 tbsp finely chopped peeled fresh ginger
1 tbsp finely chopped garlic
½ tbsp finely chopped chilli

1. Mix all the ingredients and leave to stand for 20 minutes in the fridge before serving.

Blue cheese sauce

This might sound bogging (that's nasty, for all you non-Scots), but trust me, if you're not into blue cheese then this simple, amazing sauce will convert you. It is great with chips and served as part of a selection of dips; serve it with the Parkin (see page 195) as a pud, or with my chicken wings (see page 81).

Serves 6–8

150g strong blue cheese (the stronger the better – I use Dunsyre Blue or Roquefort but Stilton would work too),
150ml single cream
lemon juice, to taste
salt and pepper

1. Place the cheese and cream in a bowl and blend with a hand blender. If you do not have a hand blender, simply crumble or grate the cheese into a bowl and work the other ingredients into it with a whisk – it will taste just as good but will have a bit of texture (I do like my sauce with a wee bit of texture to tell the truth).

2. Check the seasoning and adjust with salt, pepper and lemon juice as needed.

Index

My thanks...

To Bechan, the great woman behind this okay kind of guy. Without your support, as always, this would not have happened.

To my kids, Arrti, Balraj, Seetal and Harpreet. Thanks for not moaning too much as I have commandeered the dining table as my Book HQ; now you have it back .

To my mum and dad, my sister and my mother- and father-in-law.

To Anna-Louise Naylor-Leyland at Fork Off Management and Muna Reyal at Headline for sorting all things business and publishing. You two ROCK.

To Imogen Fortes, who had to battle with my writing style, a challenge, even after Anna-Louise and MNL had got it into normal English!

To Pene Parker for her wonderful design.

To Max and Lizzy Haarala Hamilton for the great photography (tell Coco we missed her at the shoots).

To Nicole Herft and Kat Mead for the food styling.

To the brothers for their help: Papinder 'Pindi' Singh Kusbia, Luckwinder 'Lucky' Singh Kusbia, Big Aly Stewart, Fat Dave Romanis, Erion Karaj, Colin 'Frosty' Roberts, Gavin Towart, Stewart 'B' Rough, James Hardy, Frankie Quinn, Mr Potts, Sam 'Monkey' Clarke, Stevie 'Fish' Walker, Grant and the rest of the team at Campbells Prime Meat, Paul Gunn at Wellocks and Kenny Allen at Irvines. If I have missed anyone no doubt they will punch me in the arm.

To Fiona Burrell's Edinburgh New Town Cookery School for testing out my recipes in a home environment. To all the staff and diploma students a thank you, but a huge thank you to Colette Sheridan for sorting it all out and making it work on the day.

And finally to everyone who has broken bread with me; it's what keeps me cooking.